AF715053

Media Law in Argentina

Media Law in Argentina

Agustín Siboldi
Juan Franco Raparo Faure

This book was originally published as a monograph in the International Encyclopaedia of Laws/Media Law.

Founding Editor: Roger Blanpain
General Editor: Frank Hendrickx
Volume Editors: Peggy Valcke & Eva Lievens

Wolters Kluwer

Published by:
Kluwer Law International B.V.
PO Box 316
2400 AH Alphen aan den Rijn
The Netherlands
E-mail: lrs-sales@wolterskluwer.com
Website: www.wolterskluwer.com/en/solutions/kluwerlawinternational

Sold and distributed by:
Wolters Kluwer Legal & Regulatory U.S.
920 Links Avenue
Landisville, PA 17538
United States of America
E-mail: customer.service@wolterskluwer.com

DISCLAIMER: The material in this volume is in the nature of general comment only. It is not offered as advice on any particular matter and should not be taken as such. The editor and the contributing authors expressly disclaim all liability to any person with regard to anything done or omitted to be done, and with respect to the consequences of anything done or omitted to be done wholly or partly in reliance upon the whole or any part of the contents of this volume. No reader should act or refrain from acting on the basis of any matter contained in this volume without first obtaining professional advice regarding the particular facts and circumstances at issue. Any and all opinions expressed herein are those of the particular author and are not necessarily those of the editor or publisher of this volume.

Printed on acid-free paper

ISBN 978-94-035-4008-5

e-Book: ISBN 978-94-035-4018-4
web-PDF: ISBN 978-94-035-4028-3

© 2024 Kluwer Law International BV, The Netherlands

All rights reserved. No part of this publication may be reproduced, stored in a retrieval system, or transmitted in any form or by any means, electronic, mechanical, photocopying, recording, or otherwise, without the prior written permission of the publisher.

Permission to use this content must be obtained from the copyright owner. More information can be found at: www.wolterskluwer.com/en/solutions/legal-regulatory/permissions-reprints-and-licensing

The Authors

Agustín Siboldi is a leading partner in the TMT and Antitrust practice areas at O'Farrell attorneys-at-law. He joined the firm in 1998 and has been a partner since 2007.

Mr Siboldi's practice focuses on the following areas related to economic regulation: antitrust law, both economic concentrations as well as the investigation of anticompetitive practices, telecommunication, media, and entertainment, as well as other sectors of the economy with a strong regulatory impact.

In O'Farrell, he co-leads energy areas of practice with Uriel O'Farrell and Agustina Fanelli Evans. He advises on regulatory, contractual, and litigious affairs regarding antitrust and regulatory matters in TMT, oil and gas production, power generation, natural gas and electricity transportation and distribution, as well as concession agreements breached in 2002, which led to judicial proceedings against the National State.

He represents several telecommunications and power companies in connection with regulatory and antitrust matters (Movistar, Claro Argentina, American Tower, Neutrona, Transtelco, Atis Group, EJESA—distribution company in Jujuy Province, Energía San Juan—distribution company, EDET—distribution company in Tucuman Province, EDENOR—distribution company in Buenos Aires Province, Compañía General de Electricidad, Pampa Energía, YPF Luz, Latinoamericana de Energía, FRALI, among others).

He worked as an internal counsel at Telecom Argentina Stet France Telecom S.A. between 1995 and 1998.

He has been teaching in the telecom program conducted by the *Asociación Argentina de Derecho de las Telecomunicaciones* for more than fifteen years now.

He is strongly involved in the development of renewable power generation plants as Secretary of the *Cámara Argentina de Energías Renovables*—CADER.

He holds a Bachelor's in Law from the Universidad de Buenos Aires School of Law and a Master's in Business Law from the *Escuela Superior de Economía y Administración de Empresas* ("ESEADE").

Mr Siboldi has been a professor of Economic Regulation at ESEADE for more than a decade. He is the author of an important number of publications in his fields of practice and coauthor of a renewable energy law draft jointly with the Instituto Argentina de la Energía General Mosconi.

Member of the International Bar Association (IBA) and American Bar Association (ABA).

He is a member of the *Colegio de Abogados de la Capital Federal* as well as a member of the *Colegio de Abogados de la Ciudad de Buenos Aires*.

He has been ranked by several international publications such as *Latin Lawyer*, *Chambers & Partners*, *Legal 500*, *Best Lawyers*, and *Leaders League*, among others. **Chambers Latin America**: *"Department head Agustín Siboldi is reliable and professional. I can always count on him at whatever moment, and his work is always good. He is particularly noted for his work on complex regulatory issues."*

Contact information:
Agustín Siboldi
Partner
Public Law and Economic Regulation Department +5411 4346-1087
SiboldiA@eof.com.ar

Juan Franco Raparo Faure is an Argentine attorney specializing in Constitutional and Administrative law. His practice focuses on media, telecommunication, energy, infrastructure and strongly regulated activities such as the automotive and pharmaceutical industries and financial markets.

He has developed expertise in national and international arbitration. He has also developed skills in complex litigations, especially in procedural matters related to class actions, declarative actions, state liability actions, and complex commercial litigation in local, federal, and foreign courts.

In the area of economic regulation, Juan Franco regularly advises companies in different regulated areas such as media and telecommunications, power generation—both nonrenewable and renewable—natural gas, infrastructure, administrative contracts, public utilities—electricity and gas transmission and distribution, water and sewage systems, railways—and other strongly regulated activities.

Throughout his career, Juan Franco has assisted relevant clients that participate in heavily regulated markets.

Juan Franco is currently a senior associate in Bruchou & Funes de Rioja in the Administrative Law Department. Prior to joining the firm, he used to integrate the Public Law and Economic Regulation team in O'Farrell.

He graduated with honours from the *Universidad Católica Argentina* where he also attended a postgraduate specialization degree in Administrative and Economic Law for which he was awarded with a scholarship in order to his academic background.

Juan Franco is a member of the *Colegio de Abogados de la Capital Federal*.

Contact information:
Juan Franco Raparo Faure
Senior Associate
Bruchou & Funes de Rioja
JFRF@bruchoufunes.com

Table of Contents

List of Abbreviations

ACHR	American Convention on Human Rights
ACS	Audiovisual Communication Services
ADEPA	Association of Argentine Journalism Entities—Asociación de Entidades Periodísticas Argentinas
AFSCA	Former Federal Agency for Audiovisual Communication Services—Ex Agencia Federal de Servicios de Comunicaciones Audiovisuales
AFTIC	Former Federal Agency for Information, Communication and Technology Services—Agencia Federal de Servicios de Tecnología de la Información y las Comunicaciones
AG	Attorney General
AM	Modulated Amplitude—Amplitud Modulada
AMBA	Metropolitan Area of Buenos Aires (including the City of Buenos Aires and part of the Province of Buenos Aires)—Área Múltiple Buenos Aires
CNDC	National Commission for the Defense of Competition
ENACOM	National Entity of Communications—Ente Nacional de las Comunicaciones
ENCC	National Survey on Cultural Consumption—Encuesta Nacional de Consumo Cultural
ENTIC	National Survey on Access and Use of Information and Communication Technologies—Encuesta Nacional sobre Acceso y Uso de Tecnologías de la Información y la Comunicación
FM	Modulated Frequence—Frecuencia Modulada
IACHR	Inter-American Commission on Human Rights
ICT Law	Information, Communication and Technology Services Law 27,078—Ley de Servicios de la Tecnología de la Información y las Comunicaciones 27,078
INDEC	National Institute of Statistics and Census—Instituto Nacional de Estadísticas y Censos
LDC	Law for the Defense of Competition

List of Abbreviations

Media Law 26,522	Audiovisual Communication Services Law 26,522—Ley de Servicios de Comunicaciones Audiovisuales 26,522
OECD	Organization for Economic Co-operation and Development
PBU	Mandatory Universal Basic Benefit—Prestación Básica Universal Obligatoria
PSB	Public Service Broadcasting
RTA S.E.	Radio y Televisión Argentina Sociedad del Estado
SINCA	Argentina's System of Cultural Information

Preface

This monograph aims to provide a comprehensive overview of the media landscape in Argentina, covering its political, legal, cultural, economic, and technological aspects. It is authored by Agustín Siboldi and Juan Franco Raparo Faure, both Argentine attorneys specializing in Constitutional and Administrative law, focusing on media, telecommunication and other strongly regulated activities. The monograph is based on his extensive research and experience in the field.

The monograph is divided into several chapters, each addressing a different dimension of the Argentine media system. The chapter provides a general introduction to the country's political and legal system, highlighting the constitutional and international guarantees of freedom of speech and the division of powers between the federal and provincial governments. They describe the main features of Argentine culture and society, with an emphasis on the values, diversity, and consumption patterns of the population.

The monograph intends to offer a critical and updated perspective on the challenges and opportunities that the Argentine media system faces in the context of technological convergence, market concentration, and political and social change. It also aims to contribute to the academic and professional debate on the role and regulation of the media in a democratic society, and to provide useful information and insights for media practitioners, policymakers, scholars, and students interested in the Argentine case.

General Introduction

§1. GENERAL BACKGROUND OF THE COUNTRY

I. Political and Legal System of the Country

1. Based on its Constitution, Argentina is organized as a Federal Republic divided into twenty-three Provinces and the Autonomous City of Buenos Aires with a democratic political system. The original Argentine Constitution was enacted in 1853 and amended on several occasions, the last of which was in 1994. Chapter I of Part I of the Constitution establishes a bill of rights for all individuals, Argentine or foreign, which includes the recognition and protection of life, work, commerce, liberty, equality, security, and property, publishing their ideas in the press without prior censorship, among others. Section 32 expressly sets forth: *"The Federal Congress shall not pass laws that restrict freedom of the press or establish federal jurisdiction over it."*

2. According to the Constitution, International treaties have the same hierarchy as the Constitution itself. According to sections 31 and 75 (paragraph 22) of the Argentine Constitution, international treaties, once approved by Congress and ratified by the government, take precedence over federal and provincial laws. The bilateral investment treaties signed by the federal government with most members of the Organization for Economic Co-operation and Development (OECD) grant direct rights to protect foreign investors (e.g., fair and equitable treatment, protection in the case of direct or indirect expropriation, national treatment, most favored nation treatment, etc.) and provide international arbitration (under the ICSID or UNCITRAL rules) to obtain relief for acts or omissions adopted by the Argentina Republic and any of its political subdivisions.

3. International treaties with constitutional hierarchy related to freedom of thought and speech:

- American Declaration of human being rights and obligations (Declación Americana de los Derechos y Deberes del Hombre), agreed in the IX American International Conference, Bogotá, Colombia, 1948, which Article IV states: *"Every human being has the right to freedom of investigation, of opinion and of expression and dissemination of thought by any means."*
- Universal Declaration of Human Rights (Declaración Universal de Derechos Humanos), approved by Resolution 217(III) of the General Assembly of the

United Nations, on December 10, 1948, which Article 19 states: *"Every human being has the right to freedom of opinion and expression; this right includes the right not to be disturbed because of their opinions, to investigate and receive information and opinions, and to disseminate them, without limitation of borders, by any means of expression."*
- International Convention of Human Rights agreed as part of the San José de Costa Rica Treaty (Pacto de San José de Costa Rica sobre Convención Americana de Derechos Humanos), signed on November 22, 1984; and approved by Argentina law 23,054 (Official Gazette March 27, 1984) which Article 13 sets forth the freedom of thought and speech.
- International Treaties of economic, social, cultural right, civil rights and political rights approved by Resolution 2200(XXI) of the General Assembly of the United Nations and approved by Argentina law 23,313 (Official Gazette May 13, 1986) which Article 19 sets forth the freedom of thought and speech.

4. The National Constitution, based on the checks and balances system included in the Constitution of the United States of America, has divided the federal government into three branches:

(i) The Executive Branch consisting of a person being vested with the title of President and who is elected by direct vote and may serve a maximum of two consecutive four-year terms. The Executive branch is also composed of a Vice President, the chief of Ministers and the ministers. The President promulgates or vetoes the laws sanctioned by the Congress, regulates the application of laws by sanctioning regulatory decrees and has the direction of international relations, among other powers.
(ii) The Legislative Branch under a Congress consisting of two houses, the Senate (72 members) and the Chamber of Deputies (257 members). The Congress has the power to enact laws and exercise the legislative powers delegated to the Federal Government by the Provinces (such as the enactment of Civil, Commercial, Criminal, and other Codes that apply nationwide or the approval of international treaties with foreign nations).
(iii) The Judicial Branch is vested in the Supreme Court, in courts of appeal and lower courts. The Supreme Court is composed of five members.

5. The provinces have reserved all the powers not delegated to the Federal Government by the National Constitution. Each province enacts its own Constitution, ensuring municipal autonomy and establishing its scope and content regarding the institutional, political, administrative, economic, and financial aspects.

6. Among the rights delegated to the Federal Government, we can find:

(i) The enactment of the Civil, Commercial, Criminal, Mining, Labour and Social Security Codes.
(ii) To levy indirect taxes (but this right has also been reserved by the provinces and may be exercised concurrently with the Federal Government).
(iii) The regulation of customs (which do not exist between provinces).

(iv) The creation and regulation of a Federal Bank.
(v) The regulation of commerce with foreign nations (including through the approval of international treaties).

7. The freedom of speech is expressly set forth by the National Constitution (section 32). Along the same line, the International Convention of Human Rights agreed as part of the San José de Costa Rica Treaty (Pacto de San José de Costa Rica sobre Convención Americana de Derechos Humanos), with constitutional hierarchy, establishes the freedom of thought and speech. Based upon those dispositions, federal and provincial authorities shall refrain from restricting the abovementioned rights. Apart from those constitutional rules, the Argentine legal framework includes a national media law, further analyzed below, but has not established—both at national and provincial levels—specific regulation in connection with the freedom of thought and speech.

8. Provinces may enact rules complementing the above and/or legislation of certain matters not delegated to the federal congress (i.e., official advertisement by provincial public entities, journalist registration, etc.) but always in compliance with rights and limitations set forth by the national constitution. In connection with media enterprises exceeding local jurisdiction, provinces are not entitled to set forth rules contradicting national legislation.

II. Geography and Population

9. The national population is made up of 45,376,763 inhabitants. According to the INDEC's (National Institute of Statistics and Census – *Instituto Nacional de Estadísticas y Censos*) estimations for 2023, there will be 23,103,631 women and 22,273,132 men (i.e., for every 100 females there will be 96.4 males). The population density in 2023 which accounts for sixteen persons per square kilometer (km^2). INDEC's estimation of Argentina's annual population growth rate in 2019 was 1.01%. The proportion of people below the age of 15 is estimated to be 24.44% for 2023, 63.18% between 15 and 65, and 11.79% for the age of 65 or older.

10. The population is not homogeneously distributed among the provinces:

- The Pampa region, with only 20% of the total surface, accounts for 65% of the population according to 2020 estimates.
- The Autonomous City of Buenos Aires is the most densely populated city with 15,151 inhabitants/km^2 followed by Tucumán (with 64.3 inhabitants/km^2), while the southern province of Santa Cruz only has 1.1 inhabitants/km^2.

11. Argentina is highly urbanized, with 91% of the population living in urban areas (defined as those with 2,000 inhabitants or more). Argentina's official language is Spanish, and it is spoken by the entire population in several different accents. In terms of development, the Human Development Index (HDI) published by the United Nations Development Program (UNDP) places Argentina among the countries in a very high human development category. In 2019, Argentina ranked second in Latin America and 48th in the world rank. According to OECD, the population with tertiary education is near OECD's average, 40% for some age segments and above this average for others (29% for population between 55 and 64 years old). In comparison with Latin America, Argentina shows the best results in English proficiency and has an annual average of 125,000 college graduates and 15,000 postgraduates. Regarding the educational system, in Argentina, there are 3,220 establishments in total dedicated to vocational and technical education and 131 universities in the 24 provinces. A remarkable fact is gender distribution: 61% of college graduates are female.

III. Social and Cultural Values

12. The culture of Argentina is as varied as the country's geography and is composed of a mix of ethnic groups. Modern Argentine culture has been largely influenced by Italian, Spanish, and other European immigration, while there are still less elements of Amerindian and African origin and influence, particularly in the fields of music and art. Buenos Aires, its cultural capital, is largely characterized by both the prevalence of people of European descent and European styles in architecture. Museums, cinemas, and galleries are abundant in all the large urban centers, as well as traditional establishments such as literary bars or bars offering live music of a variety of genres.[1]

13. Argentine values are a shared identity core that brings together actions and thoughts aimed at increasing social capital and fostering the common good among Argentines. Argentine values intend to create a community formed by all those who are convinced that Argentina is a great country. Argentina is a collective country where its values focus on diversity and solidarity. In addition to being a collectivistic society. The Argentines are from traditional customs but are also kind and friendly. The greeting is a crucial element in the Argentine culture where we see that nobody leaves without being greeted; Men kiss women, Women kiss men, and other men kiss men on the cheek. Another principal value for Argentines is the family. In Argentina, for example, it is prevalent for family members to visit traditionally on Sunday, meetings in which there are music, food, and games. Apart from these types of meetings, the family meets for family events or gatherings such as births, weddings, and similar activities.[2]

14. Argentina has a detailed literary history and is one of the region's most active publishing industries. Argentine writers have figured prominently in Latin American literature, since becoming a fully united entity in the 1850s, with a strong constitution and a defined nation-building plan. The struggle between the Federalists (who favored a loose confederation of provinces based on rural conservatism)

1. Downloaded from Wikipedia on Nov. 27, 2020, https://en.wikipedia.org/wiki/Culture_of_Argentina.
2. Downloaded from Wikipedia on Nov. 27, 2020, https://en.wikipedia.org/wiki/Culture_of_Argentina.

and the Unitarians (pro-liberalism and advocates of a strong central government that would encourage European immigration) set the tone for Argentine literature of the time.

15. The ideological divide between gaucho epic Martín Fierro by José Hernández and Facundo by Domingo Faustino Sarmiento is a great example. Hernández, a federalist, was opposed to the centralizing, modernizing, and Europeanizing tendencies. Sarmiento wrote in support of immigration as the only way to save Argentina from becoming subject to the rule of a small number of dictatorial caudillo families, arguing such immigrants would make Argentina more modern and open to Western European influences and therefore a more prosperous society. Argentine literature of that period was fiercely nationalist. It was followed by the modernist movement, which emerged in France in the late nineteenth century, and this period in turn was followed by vanguardism, with Ricardo Güiraldes as an important reference. Jorge Luis Borges, its most acclaimed writer, found new ways of looking at the modern world in metaphor and philosophical debate, and his influence has extended to writers all over the globe. Borges is most famous for his works in short stories, such as Fictions and The Aleph. Some of the nation's notable writers, poets, and intellectuals include Juan Bautista Alberdi, Jorge Luis Borges, Roberto Arlt, Enrique Banchs, Adolfo Bioy Casares, Silvina Bullrich, Eugenio Cambaceres, Julio Cortázar, Esteban Echeverría, Leopoldo Lugones, Eduardo Mallea, Ezequiel Martínez Estrada, Tomás Eloy Martínez, Victoria Ocampo, Manuel Puig, Ernesto Sabato, Osvaldo Soriano, Alfonsina Storni, María Elena Walsh and Oliverio Girondo.[3]

16. Argentineans differ from one another. Geography might have an influence on the characteristics of people you may be in contact with. For instance, people from a metropolitan city, such as Buenos Aires, are generally more informal and direct than people from towns and provinces of the interior of the country. Another issue is the way to talk with people. In a formal conversation, people refer to others using the personal pronoun "usted." This voice is used especially when young people are addressing an old person. However, "vos" (equivalent "tú," the most common voice in Spanish) is widely used among young people and among friends. Also, in employee relationship based on trust and more direct contact, the use of "vos" is most common. Trust is important to determine the use of the voice.

17. At first contact, people are willing to talk about work and social tastes; in an urban area, people are less willing to address personal issues. Although Argentine people are family-oriented; in smaller communities, people tend to address family issues more immediately and personally compared to those in big cities. For example, "what is your family like?," "how many kids do you have?," etc. Generally speaking, Argentineans are open-minded and outgoing. All issues can be addressed in a conversation. However, at first contact, religion and political issues should be avoided or addressed politely and with some restraint. Regarding public displays of affection, some emotions are acceptable because people are willing to

3. Downloaded from Wikipedia on Nov. 27, 2020, https://en.wikipedia.org/wiki/Culture_of_Argentina.

express themselves in a more open way than is customary in parts of the world. Mostly, it is women who are allowed expressions of affection, especially in informal situations.

18. In connection with workplace environment, styles differ between workplaces, but it is important to be clean and punctual. Argentines pay extreme attention to dressing, both in summer and winter. At the workplace, men must wear formal jackets. Women are expected to wear appropriate clothing at work (Argentine women pay a lot of attention to fashion issues and style. Beauty details and ornaments are allowed and sometimes expected at workplace). Colleagues and even supervisors are often addressed by their first names. Sometimes, in a hierarchical relationship, the use of Dr or Licenciado is expected. People are expected to meet deadlines in the workplace, although there is often some degree of flexibility. However, at some social events (which may involve work issues), people are often much less punctual. Generally speaking, people like to start social events late and they enjoy staying out late too. Work schedules differ from one workplace to another. For instance, in public service, people have a routine of 9 a.m. to 5 p.m. However, in private companies, employees can work earlier or later. A tendency to be accountable for results is more used in private sector than in public sector.

19. Regarding religion, class, ethnicity and gender:[4]

- Gender: In recent decades, women have gained access to many positions in the job market as well as in politics, economics, etc. However, some constraints keep women from advancing within a more predominantly male job culture and help explain the small numbers of women at the top level of many organizations.
- Religion: Generally speaking, Argentina is a Catholic country, with the presence of some minorities of, Jewish (2% of the population, concentrated in the area of Buenos Aires) and other minorities such as Muslims. There is no religious cleavage in Argentina, and religion does not usually have any particular impact on the workplace.
- Class: Class differences do not have a specific impact on workplace.
- Ethnicity: 85% of the population in Argentina is of European origin, and 15% are of mixed origins. Sometimes, discrimination due to physical appearance does arise.

§2. The Media Landscape

I. Overview of Media Markets and Main Actors

20. The media market in Argentine shows high levels of concentration in a few companies that dominate the relevant industries. This concentration process may have started in the 1990s when the television signals which used to belong to the Government were transferred to privates and, in that context, the first multimedia

4. Downloaded from Wikipedia on Nov. 27, 2020, https://en.wikipedia.org/wiki/Culture_of_Argentina.

groups were formed, headed by national capital mainly coming from the printed media sector. This crossover between the graphic journalistic sector and the audio-visual sector seems to have been the starting point for the formation of large media conglomerates.

21. In Argentine media markets, the same economic groups own different types of media companies; the same company that owns newspapers also dominates print media, radio, television, online press, etc. There is a high geographic concentration, considering that the main information and entertainment centers are in the metropolitan area of Buenos Aires (*Área Múltiple Buenos Aires* (AMBA)). Also, there is a strong vertical concentration, considering that the economic groups that produce media content also control the companies in charge of their distribution.

22. According to the research published by Media Ownership Monitor Argentina,[5] TV is the most popular news medium in the country, according to the most recent and representative surveys. Only in the AMBA, where ratings are measured, the four leading TV groups (including free and pay TV channels) account for 56.7% of the market. As the content created in Buenos Aires is usually repeated in the other provinces of Argentina, the four groups' market share is supposedly even higher at a national level. The main groups that operate in the TV industry are Clarín and Viacom.

23. Printed media has lost its direct influence on readership due to a dramatic decline in sales. Nevertheless, it still plays a key role in agenda-setting for radio stations, TV channels and digital news portals, many of which belong to the same media groups. Concentration in print media is higher than in TV. The four leading business groups, to which the highest circulation newspapers belong, account for 74.81% of sales. Grupo Clarín alone covers 43% of the market.

24. Concentration is also high in radio, a sector that is comprised of a huge number of radio stations thanks to its technological architecture. The four main business groups (the largest being Clarín, Indalo and PRISA/Albavisión) account for 53% of the audience.

25. In contrast to print, online newspapers are experiencing a surge in visits. The tendency towards concentration in this segment is similar to others, against the popular belief that the internet fosters diversity in the use and consumption of information and therefore democratizes the design of the public agenda. Although it is impossible to determine the total number of visits to news websites and to estimate the percentage of concentration, the more concentrated media companies stand out in rankings that classify websites based on their number of visitors. Among the six

5. *See* Media Ownership Monitor, *"Main media groups: an overview,"* available at http://argentina.mom-gmr.org/en/findings/concentration/. That data is also confirmed by the Argentine regulator authority, according to the stats provided on its official website: https://www.enacom.gob.ar/indicadores-de-mercado_p2877.

informative digital media outlets with the largest audience, four belong to Grupo Clarín: Clarín.com, TN.com.ar, Cien radios and La Voz del Interior.

26. Reporters Without Borders' research includes an indicator that measures cross-media audience concentration. It is a temporary indicator that can be implemented while expecting markets to begin reporting their operations more transparently. Yet, the collected data show that cross-media concentration accounts for 59.24% of total concentration in the hands of eight leading media groups:

(1) Grupo Clarín: 25.28% (6.84% in radio, 10.62% in TV, and 7.82% in print).
(2) Grupo América: 7.25% (2.27% in radio, 4.09% in TV, and 0.89% in print).
(3) VIACOM: 7.10% in TV.
(4) Grupo Indalo: 6.62% (5.12% in radio and 1.5% in TV).
(5) PRISA-Albavisión: 6.21% (4.33% in radio and 1.88% in TV).
(6) La Nación: 2.97% in print.
(7) Cadena 3: 2.6% in radio.
(8) Federal System of Media and Public Content (SFMyCP, National Government) 1.65% in TV.[6]

27. The most relevant actor in the media marks is *Grupo Clarín*. Clarín was founded in 1945 by Roberto Noble, a politician at the time and has grown into other media and industries since the 1980s under the management of the group's controlling shareholder and CEO, Héctor Magnetto. After the merger of Grupo Clarín's Cablevisión (the largest cable TV operator) and Telecom (one of the main landline and mobile telephony companies) in 2018, the gap between the conglomerate and the rest of the media has widened in terms of income, audience, geographical scope of the group's operations and its controlling position in each market. For instance, even without taking into consideration its cable TV, mobile and landline telephony, and internet access operations, Grupo Clarín reported revenues worth USD 159 million in 2017, while each of its competitors had a turnover below USD 10 million. The group's revenues are considerably higher including the other business units of Cablevisión holding.

28. In addition, Grupo Clarín is the group that benefits the most from official advertising, both from the National Government and the provincial governments.

29. After Grupo Clarín and Fintech announced their merger in June 2017, the services provided by Cablevisión and Telecom together accounted for 42% of landline services, 34% of mobile, 56% of broadband internet access, 35% of mobile internet access and 40% of pay TV.[7] The merger constituted a violation of the law that regulates spectrum (the mobile telephony electromagnetic bandwidth). In addition, Cablevisión-Telecom received privileges in the operation of fixed line phone

6. *See* Media Ownership Monitor, *"Main media groups: an overview,"* available at http://argentina.mom-gmr.org/en/findings/concentration/.
7. *See* data provided by the Argentine antitrust authority, *"Comisión Nacional de Defensa de la Competencia,"* available at http://cndc.produccion.gob.ar/node/2573.

and Internet infrastructure, particularly the communications backbone network in the center and north part of Argentina—the country's most populated areas.

30. Grupo Clarín has been at the center of another merger in the past already: in December 2007, Néstor Kirchner, the President of Argentina at the time, "authorized" the group's commercial exploitation of the two largest cable operators in the country, Multicanal and Cablevisión.

31. The merger between Cablevisión and Telecom which took place in 2017 consolidated the communications policy strategy adopted by former President Mauricio Macri (2015–2019). Despite some occasional erratic behavior, Macri's administration proved very effective in adapting State regulations and policies to cater to the needs of the largest communication conglomerate in the country.

32. Grupo Clarín's growing concentration of media resources, to the disadvantage of other media, has also had a negative impact on the symbolic and economic influence of its competitors. A concern in all sectors of the economy, banned by Article 42 of Argentina's National Constitution, concentration is particularly detrimental in the information and communication industries. In this regard, international and national case law on freedom of expression defines excessive concentration as a device of indirect censorship that violates the right to freedom of expression and the right of access to culture.

33. Concentration results in a decrease in information sources (with less plurality of sources), standardizes genres and entertainment formats (thus attacking content diversity), prioritizes certain styles and topics, and reduces the scope of topics and formats. Besides, media concentration usually leads to a single and prevailing editorial line. It is hard to find truly disagreeing views on sensitive issues within a single media group.

34. Another effect of concentration is the geographical centralization of information and content production in the cities where a group's headquarters are located, a key feature of the Argentine media system.

35. In addition, concentration also negatively impacts the labor market and the journalistic profession at large. Some media outlets have been closed down, while others have merged, thus leading to economies of scale, cost savings and layoffs. In addition, within a highly concentrated media system, due to the increasing concentration of the industry, journalists have very few chances of finding a good job once they dare to confront any of the leading media groups.

36. As a result, and with only a few exceptions, concentration processes tend to weaken the free circulation of ideas in a society. For several decades, concentrated actors have played a dominant role in the design of the public policy agenda of the information and communication industries in different countries with different regulatory systems. Unfortunately, those trends are still ongoing and the Argentine media market is highly concentrated.

II. Broadcasting Infrastructure

37. About the equipment and infrastructure in Argentine households, Argentina's INDEC reports that power supply penetration is almost universal (98.8%). By 2017, 64.3% of households had a computer. In addition, 75.9% of households also had some type of Internet connection.[8] The last National Survey on Access and Use of Information and Communication Technologies (*Encuesta Nacional sobre Acceso y Uso de Tecnologías de la Información y la Comunicación* (ENTIC)),[9] which was carried out in 2015, showed that 97.7% of all Argentine households had a TV, while 75.5% had a radio receiver.

38. In 2017, average Internet connection speed over fixed broadband was 12 Mbps, even though twenty-one out of the country's twenty-four provinces registered lower speeds. The main Internet connection device is a cable modem (48.5%), followed by Asimetric Digital Suscriber Line (ADSL) (45.5%) and, to a considerably lesser extent, optical fiber (2.7%).

39. Data from Argentina's National Entity of Communications (ENACOM, by its initial in Spanish) shows that in every hundred households, seventy have a fixed telephony line, seventy have a pay TV subscription and sixty-one have Internet access over fixed broadband. Private estimates, such as those made by consulting agency Business Bureau, indicate that pay TV penetration is close to 80%, given the fact that there are prepaid subscription systems and tapped or hacked connections. In addition, the number of mobile telephony lines is higher than that of Argentina's population: 140 lines for every 100 inhabitants. What is more, of every hundred households, ninety-seven have a TV receiver and seventy-six have an AM/FM radio receiver.[10]

40. The National Survey on Cultural Consumption (*Encuesta Nacional de Consumo Cultural* (ENCC))[11] is carried out by Argentina's System of Cultural Information (SINCA) and provides information on Argentines' media use based on their answers to the survey. According to the 2017 edition, radio has been one of the most affected traditional media, having lost 17% of its share in comparison to the results of the previous survey in 2013. However, its penetration still is high (70%). The traditional radio receiver continues to be the most popular device (62%), followed by the car stereo receiver (24%) and the cell phone (22%).

41. TV continued to have a high penetration rate in Argentines' cultural life in 2017, with a traditional TV reach of 95%. However, data suggest that the TV set

8. *See* INDEC, data available in https://www.indec.gob.ar/indec/web/Institucional-Indec-InformesTecnicos-71.
9. *See* INDEC, data available in https://www.indec.gob.ar/indec/web/Institucional-Indec-InformesTecnicos-71.
10. *See* INDEC, data available in https://www.indec.gob.ar/indec/web/Institucional-Indec-InformesTecnicos-71.
11. https://encuestadeconsumo.sinca.gob.ar/.

also became the fastest-growing means of Internet connection between 2013 and 2017, and smart TVs accounted for 54% of market penetration in 2017.

42. Like radio, printed media is one of the industries that is losing momentum. In 2013, 73% of those surveyed read newspapers; in 2017, this figure decreased to 57%. According to respondents, the main cause of the fall is a lack of interest. Like radio, the decline among young people is sharper than among elder adults.

43. Below is some relevant data on those media outlets with the largest number of listeners, readers or viewers. Grupo Clarín controls many rankings in different industries: Radio Mitre is the leading Modulated Amplitude (AM) radio station; La 100 leads the Modulated Frequence (FM) radio segment; Clarín is the broadest circulation newspaper in the country and its website is the second most visited news website; Clarín's Canal 13 is the second most viewed open TV channel; and Clarín's TN is the pay TV channel with the highest rating in the country.[12]

44. However, it is still possible to find a few more and less relevant market actors besides the all-dominating market position of Clarín. La Nacion's readership is leading in the printed and online media industries; Grupo Indalo shows a good performance in pay TV (with the second most viewed channel, C5N), in radio (Radio 10 and Radio Pop are among the leading stations) and in web (the website Minutouno is among those with largest numbers of visitors); Grupo América owns América TV, which is one of the most viewed free TV channels, and their radio is popular in Buenos Aires and Mendoza. VIACOM is a media company that only operates in the (pay and free) TV sector: Telefé is the most viewed free TV channel.

45. According to ENCC, in 2017, the main device to access Internet was the cell phone (76%), followed by the computer (57%). Cell phones are used to listen to music (50%), listen to the radio (17%), read newspapers (14%) and play video games (12%). As regards social media, the most popular in Argentina were Facebook (64%), Instagram (27%) and Twitter (13%). Besides, in audiovisual content, free websites such as YouTube were the third most viewed platforms (31.5%), after cable TV (74%) and free TV (58%). Paid streaming services such as Netflix ranked forth, with 25% of respondents using them.[13]

46. In terms of supply, current statistics in Argentina are not specific enough to accurately determine the number of media and news producers. According to data gathered by SINCA in their cultural map[14] of Argentina, there are 2,130 radio stations, 56 free TV channels, 191 printed newspapers and 322 digital news outlets.

---

12. *See* Media Ownership Monitor Argentina, *"Media Consumption,"* 2018.
13. *See*, ENCC official website, https://www.enacom.gob.ar/institucional/mas-de-200--de-incremento-en-el-acceso-a-internet-de-fibra-optica-en-toda-la-argentina_n4455#:~:text=Crece%20el%20acceso%20a%20Internet&text=En%20ese%20sentido%2C%20la%20tasa,hogares%20con%20acceso%20a%20Internet.
14. *See*, SINCA, data available at https://www.sinca.gob.ar/mapa.aspx.

47. In their records, ENACOM lists 6,125 radio stations (including 279 AM radio stations) with license or authorization awarded by the State, while they estimate that there are around 5,000 illegal radio stations. In addition, according to this record, in which all media must register, there are 117 active pay TV channels across the country. The list also includes 111 registered free TV channels in Argentina.

48. The news agency sector is small: there are two national agencies (State-owned Télam and private-owned Noticias Argentinas) that compete with large international agencies such as Reuters and Agence France-Presse (AFP).

III. Technological and Economic Developments in the Media Markets

A. *Television and Telecommunication Markets: Historical Division and Evolution*

49. Argentina's physical networks deployed for rendering both telecommunications and television are largely digitalized, a process which became possible at the beginning of the 1990s. Said digitalization is currently completed when referring to physical networks. On the contrary, the spectrum allocated to pay television—historically known as broadcasting (*radiodifusión*)—is notoriously behind schedule in comparison with OECD—and neighboring countries. One can speculate that television and telecommunication physical network operators have been able to compete since the end of the 1990s and the beginning of the 2000s. Nevertheless, convergence between telecommunication and television physical network operators was only and suddenly authorized by the end of 2017, beginning—with certain restrictions—on January 1, 2018.

B. *Television and Telecommunications Markets Were Still Segregated Even under the New Legal Framework for Media Market Enacted by Law in 2009*

50. Until then, telecommunications operators in general (either via physical or spectrum-based networks) were forbidden from rendering television, be it satellite, through physical or air networks. Meanwhile, in the same period, all television operators, regardless of the technologies they would resort to, were allowed to enter the telecommunication market, giving room for quite an extraordinary one-sided convergence process, where television operators may compete with telecommunication operators, while the later were forbidden to compete in the television market (among others: Decree 62/90, Official Gazette January 12, 1990; Decree 764/00, Official Gazette September 5, 2000, which expressly contemplated the one-sided convergence referred to in this paragraph). Said scheme was kept by relatively recent Audiovisual Communication Services Law 26,522(*Ley de Servicios de Comunicaciones Audiovisuales 26,522* (Media Law 26,522)) (sections 25 and others; Official Gazette, October 10, 2009—"Media Law").

C. *New Legal Framework of Telecommunication Enacted by Law in 2014*

51. Argentina only initiated the process to allow the convergence between television and telecommunications markets with the enactment of Information, Communication and Technology Services Law 27,078 (Official Gazette, December 19, 2014—"ICT Law"). Nevertheless, section 9 of the law prohibited the telecommunication operator from rendering satellite television.

52. ICT Law also sets forth a transition regimen aimed at granting the conditions needed for the assurance of competition by taking into account the following parameters (section 94):

(a) Establishment of promotion zones for limited terms within which Telecommunications Operators with significant market power may not provide television services.
(b) Promotion and protection of the so-called community networks, guaranteeing that the conditions of their exploitation respond to the technical, economic, and social needs of the community.
(c) Establishment of incentives for the deployment of regional infrastructure and strengthening of local actors such as: allocation of universal service funds, ease of access to financing and investment, ease of access to public works programs, tax advantages, and advice on technology and innovation, among others.
(d) Establishment of regulatory asymmetries as instruments of universalization aimed at the development of effective competition, determining a set of different rights and duties for one provider with respect to another, even when both act in the same geographic market, providing equivalent services in the aforementioned, between other assumptions, to the conditions for the entry of new providers, for the establishment of limits to the concentration and the expansion of the service provision area.

53. Moreover, ICT Law sets forth two additional conditions for the telecommunications operators entering the television market (section 95):

(a) If the license is required for the provision of television services and there is another provider in the same service area, the Media Law Enforcement Authority, in each specific case, must carry out a comprehensive evaluation of the request that considers the interest of the population and request a binding opinion from the Competition Law Authority that establishes the conditions of provision that must be applied in the award of the license.
(b) In order to obtain the television services license, the applicant, in addition to complying with the provisions established in Media Law, if applicable, must abide by the promotion deadlines set forth in subsection a) of Article 94 of this law, referred to above.

54. After the enactment of the ICT Law, as set forth in the abovementioned paragraphs, television networks were subject to the Media Law while telecommunication operator networks were regulated by ICT Law, even though, from a technical point of view, both were digitalized networks able to provide either television or telecommunication services.

55. We will provide more detailed and general views about the legal framework of the media and telecommunications in the following sections.

D. Media Law and Telecommunications Laws Were Extensively Amended in 2015 Through a Decree of Necessity and Urgency Enacted by the Executive Power with the Same Hierarchy as a Formal Law

56. Under the legal framework described above, while the "transition regimen" set forth by it was still pending regulation, the new administration led by former President Mauricio Macri enacted a Necessity and Urgency Decree (*Decreto de Necesidad y Urgencia* 267/15, which is furnished with the same hierarchy of a law enacted from the National Congress) (Official Gazette December 23, 2015) profoundly amended media and telecommunications laws. Among a number of changes, following a brief detail of the most relevant ones for the purpose of this analysis:

(a) It ratifies the convergence of the media and telecommunications markets in terms of network service providers and innovates by submitting to the ICT Law the television network services previously governed by the Media Law.
In both cases, these are services whose characterizing element is the use of digital telecommunication networks. The regulatory goal was to subject all telecommunications networks that would technically be able to compete with each other to the same regulatory framework, the ICT Law.

(b) Establishment of the rules for access to the television market by the licensees of telecommunication services (namely "Information Technology and Communications Services,") previously delegated to the National Executive Power, and reduction of the discretion within which such measures could be defined.
By modifying Articles 94 and 95 of the ICT Law, Decree 267/15 introduces important changes in the "transition regime" towards the convergence of television and telecommunication markets.
Indeed, it establishes that: (i) the providers resulting from the privatization of the former state-owned telecommunication company, namely, ENTEL under Decree 62/90, i.e., Telecom and Telefónica; (ii) the providers that had been developed within the framework of the tetra-polio established by Decree 264/98 (Official Gazette March 13, 1998) for the transition stage towards competition, i.e., today Telecom (in the south), Telefónica (in the north), Telmex Argentina and Movistar (throughout the country) and; (iii) the providers of the Mobile Telephone Service (MTS) licensed under Resolution 575/93 of the Ministry of Economy, Public Works and Services of the Nation (Official Gazette

June 17, 1993), i.e., Personal, Movistar and Claro; they may only provide television services (namely, "subscription broadcasting services"), by any means, as of January 1, 2018, a period that Enforcement Authority (ENACOM) may extend until January 1, 2019 (ICT Law, Article 94). The described temporary restrictions were applicable to direct and indirect shareholders of the subjects affected by it, as well as to companies in which they have direct or indirect shareholding or some type of associative contract other than companies (ICT Law, Article 96; according to Decree 267/15).

Consequently, the telecommunications licensees not included in the abovementioned restrictions were able to provide television services immediately (previous obtention of the corresponding license). Among the licensees who are not covered by the aforementioned temporal restriction, it is possible to identify both incumbent television service providers that had already entered the telecommunications market—such as Telecentro—as well as telecommunications licensees developed within the framework of the competition in the telecommunications sector, such as Impsat or Fibertel.

Nevertheless, completely unexpectedly and without any explicit ground, satellite television licensees were still forbidden to render telecommunications services (by maintaining Article 9, second paragraph of the ICT Law, and extending it by modifying Article 45 of the Media Law, Article 45, paragraph 1, item a).

(c) Ratification of the restriction for joint control of television services operators in public service providers.

Beyond the transition conditions towards convergence that have been described above, Decree 267/15 maintains the historical restriction on participation in the capital stock of providers of television services—now governed by the ICT Law—by companies that are holders of a concession or license that authorizes them to provide a public service (i.e., electricity and natural gas transportation and distribution), granted by the State, be it at the national, provincial or municipal level (Articles 95 and 96; Decree 267/15). This restriction is extended to its shareholders with 10% or more of the right to vote to form the corporate will—nothing changes up to that point—and to the companies holding "any direct or indirect social participation" in these shareholders and in the holding companies of said license, as well as any type of collaboration, organization, participation or community contract with people or Companies.

(d) Ratification that the satellite television services are still governed by the Media Law and, therefore, telecommunications providers are not entitled to provide satellite television.

After having ordered that television services by physical link and by radio link be subjected to the ICT Law, replacing the Media Law (according to new Articles 6, 19 and releated articules of the ICT Law), ratifies that "subscription broadcasting services" through satellite resources will continue to be subject to the Media Law (Article 38, according to Decree 267/15). In turn, this implies the separation of satellite television services, subjected to the Media Law, from television services rendered via any other technology, subjected to the ICT Law, which prohibits telecommunications service providers from providing satellite television services, without any technical or regulatory support.

(e) Flexibility of the regime of extension of licenses for the provision of television services.

Decree 267/15 eliminates the restriction of a single extension for a period of ten years to incorporate the possibility of successive extensions. Thus, the licenses for the provision of television services of the Media Law will be subject to a first five-year extension that will be automatic if the interested party submits a request to ENACOM with a notice of between twelve and six months before its expiration. Exceptionally and prior to technical opinion, the validity of the licenses may be extended in advance (Media Law, Article 40, according to Decree 267/15).

The subsequent extensions will be for a period of ten years, unless the relevant authority decides to call new licensees to tender, in the terms of Article 32 of the Media Law (not modified by Decree 267/15), based on reasons of public interest, the introduction of new technologies or compliance with international agreements. In this case, the affected licensees will not have any acquired right to their license (Media Law, Article 40, according to Decree 267/15).

It should be remembered that the Media Law originally provided that after an initial extension of ten years, a new competition would be carried out—in all cases—without prejudice to the right of the affected licensee to participate in it. Decree 267/2015 came to transform into an exception to what was the principle under the original Media Law.

(f) Elimination of the nontransferability of television services licenses.

It eliminates the nontransferable nature of the licenses for the provision of television services originally provided for by the Media Law, replacing it with the requirement that the eventual transferee or new owner meet the admissibility conditions established for its award.

As in the case of ICT service licenses, Decree 267/2015, by modifying Article 41 of the Media Law (Article 16), provides for (i) ex post notification within thirty days of the transaction completion; (ii) that the transfer of licenses and shareholdings will be considered made ad referendum of ENACOM; and (iii) that the authorizations will be considered fully issued if ENACOM has not denied them within ninety days of receiving the notification of the transaction. In case of registering observations to the presentation made by the interested party, the term will be counted from the moment they have been corrected. Contracts subject to ENACOM approval may not be executed until they receive express or tacit approval, under the terms of the new Article 41 of the Media Law. Failure to comply with this limitation will constitute a cause for the expiration of the license in question, with prior notice from ENACOM.

Although it does not expressly establish it, ENACOM's authorization does not replace that of the enforcement authority of the Competition Law 27,442 (Official Gazette May 15, 2018).

(g) Reduction of the limitations to the possession of multiple television services licenses under the Media Law. Ratification of restrictions that prevent concentrating satellite television services and with ICT Services and their extension to services under Media Law.

Decree 267/15 expands the number of television services licenses that can be controlled by a single person to fifteen licenses (Media Law, Article 45, section

1, paragraph a), according to Decree 267/15). Before, there were ten and they included other modalities such as radio link provision, thus aggravating the limitation. Likewise, the restriction to a content signal originally contained in the Media Law is eliminated, as well as the one that limited to twenty-four licenses of broadcasting services by subscription with physical links in different locations and that other that established an audience limit at 35% of the total inhabitants of the country or subscribers of the service in question (Media Law, Article 45, section 1, sections b) and c), according to of Decree 267/15).
Finally, it eliminates any limitation regarding the quantity of signals that can be concentrated by a television services licensee under the Media Law. It should be remembered that the Media Law originally provided that national providers could only be holders of a unique television signal, while television network providers could not be holders of television signals, with the exception of a signal of its own generation (Media Law, Article 45, section 3, before Decree 267/15).

(h) Relaxation of the limitations for linking stations in networks.
In relation to the constitution of radio and television networks, the Media Law allows their formation by maintaining the requirement that such a link recognize a time limit, without specifying one, modifying the following rules: (i) the programming to be repeated may not exceed 30% in city with more than 1.5 million inhabitants and 40% in the others (previously a single limit of 30% was foreseen); (ii) said percentages are applied to the monthly programming—not to the daily, as originally established by the Media Law—which gives the related stations the possibility of allocating the programming to weekends, where—except for the case of sporting events—local programming offers are reduced and; (iii) it eliminates the restriction of the linking of radio stations in networks to providers of the same type and class of service (Media Law, Article 63, according to Decree 267/15).
Otherwise, it maintains the following guidelines: (iv) maintain 100% control of the contracting rights for advertising; (v) as well as a local and own news service in central hours; (vi) maintain the possibility of a higher proportion of programming repetition for specific cases, with the prior approval of ENACOM in the event that the assignment of multiple headers for the production of content to be broadcast is verified; (vii) providers of different types may agree to retransmission of programs up to 10% of their programming, even with respect to the same areas of provision (aspect in which the decree innovates) and; (viii) for events of relevant interest, the formation of open radio and television networks is allowed without any limitation (Media Law, Article 63, according to Decree 267/15).

(i) It repeals provisions of the Media Law that are inconsistent with the criteria incorporated by Decree 267/15:
   - Requirement of a single and exclusive corporate purpose: The requirement established in subsection c) of Article 31 of the Media Law (television services under Media Law had to be provided through companies with a single corporate purpose).

The elimination of this requirement is complemented by the obligation to generate business units for the provision of television services in a segregated manner under the Media Law and ICT services under the ICT Law, carrying out separate accounting on a mandatory basis. This is the result of the requirements of Article 95 of the ICT Law, modified by Decree 267/15.

- Application of the institute of *"assets assigned to the provision"* ("bienes afectados a la prestación de servicios"): The definition contained in Article 43 of the Media Law, which identified those goods "essential" for the provision of the service in question, considering *"such those that are detailed in the bidding documents and conditions and in the award proposals as minimum equipment of each station and the elements that are incorporated as replacement or re-equipment."* The assets thus identified could only be sold or encumbered as long as it was necessary in order to improve the service and had the prior authorization of the relevant authority.

This legal institute has strong roots in the notion of public services, applicable when they are provided—via concession—by individuals, so that within the expiration of the term of the concession contract or license, the goods necessary for the provision of the service revert in favor of the granting State (which could apply them again to the provision of the public service in question or give them again in concession for a new actor to carry out the same). This concept remains fully valid in all those infrastructure sectors that are still considered "natural monopolies," i.e., transportation and distribution services of gas and electricity, in which the validity of this institute is clearly justified by the fact that without the possibility of recovering the assets necessary for the provision of such services, they could not meet the continuity requirement of a public service that satisfies a basic need of citizens, such as the cases mentioned above.

- "Non-delegability" of the distribution of television services under the Media Law: The *"non-delegability"* established by subsection e) of Article 44 of the Media Law is eliminated, which was a correlate of the requirement—which remains—that the exploitation of the television license under the Media Law is in charge of their holders. Thus, the prohibition on *"Delegating the distribution of audiovisual communication services to a third party"* is repealed.

Licenses: Eliminates Article 48 of the Media Law, since this article provided the control of compliance with the limits to the concentration of television licenses under the Media Law, to the extent that Decree 267/2015 establishes a new control mechanism in this regard, which we have commented above, now included in Article 95 and concordant of the Media Law, modified by Decreee 267/2015.

- Determination of the contents of *"open television broadcasting services"*: Thus, repeals the requirement to have at least 60% of the programming produced locally and at least 30% of its own production that includes local news programs is eliminated by repealing Article 65, second paragraph (which we interpret refers to point 2 of said article), of the Media Law.

The qualification of "public services" that the ICT Law assigned to ICT Services: repeals Article 15 of the ICT Law that established *"the essential and strategic public service character of Information and Communication Technologies*

(ICT) in competition with the use and access to telecommunications networks, for and between licensees of ICT Services."

The power of the relevant authority to establish tariffs for the provision of ICT services: In line with the aforementioned "despublication" and with the repeal of the application of the institute of *"assets affected to the provision of public services,"* the relevant authority's right to set tariff for the provision ICT services considered "public services" (those determined by the relevant authority for reasons of "public interest"; former Article 48 of the ICT Law).

(j) It repeals provisions of the ICT Law that are inconsistent with the criteria incorporated by Decree 267/15:

- Enforcement authority—Former Federal Agency for Audiovisual Communication Services (AFSCA) ("Agencia Federal de Servicios de Comunicaciones Audiovisuales"): Eliminates Articles 10, 12, 13 and 14 of the Media Law that—respectively—created the AFSCA, established its nature and address, budget, and composition of its board of directors; while the validity of Article 12, which establishes its missions and functions, is now in charge of ENACOM.

Federal Council of Audiovisual Communication ("Consejo Federal de Comunicación Audiovisual"): Repeals Articles 15 and 16 of the Media Law that created said Council and established its integration.

- Former Federal Agency for Information, Communication and Technology Services (AFTIC) ("Agencia Federal de Servicios de Tecnología de la Información y las Comunicaciones") enforcement authority: repeals Articles 77 and 78 of the ICT Law, which created the AFTIC and established its nature and domicile, respectively, while maintaining Articles 79 to 81, which establish that ENACOM—before—the AFTIC—it is the continuator of the Communications Secretariat ("Secretaría de Comunicaciones") and the National Communications Commission ("Comisión Nacional de Comunicaciones"), functions and powers of the ICT Law enforcement authority.
- It also repeals Articles 82 to 86 of the ICT Law, which established: (i) the control of the AFTIC by the General Audit Office of the Nation and the General Auditor of the Nation, the obligation to disclose the acts of the directory, resources, appointments and hiring (Article 82); (ii) defined the integration of its budget (Article 83); (iii) determined the integration of its board of directors (Article 84); (iv) created the Federal Council for Telecommunications Technologies and Digitalization ("Consejo Federal de Tecnologías de la Información y las Comunicaciones") (Article 85) and established its composition (Article 86).

E. Criteria, Paradigms, and Principles Adopted by the Media and ICT Laws as Amended by Decree 267/15

57.

(i) Maintains a regime inspired by "competition by services" criterion (as opposed to "competition by networks"), based upon the network sharing obligation as a way of developing competition in the absence of competitive networks, as already provided for in Decree 764/00 and kept by the ICT Law.

(ii) In parallel, the amendments to the Media and ICT Laws set forth specific obligations on the telecommunications providers.
In this sense, it allows telecommunication operators to render television signal distribution services in competition with the incumbent television cable operators (which under the previous media law were protected from telecommunications providers' competition).
In connection with telecommunications, infrastructure sets rules making mandatory sharing them with competitors (poles, columns, structures, rights of way and any kind of installation over which telecommunication cables and equipment may be deployed; Media Law, Article 6).

(iii) Clearly divides the subject matters of the ICT and Media Laws: ICT Law focuses on the transmission, administration, management, request, and delivery of information service, that is, on information and communications technology, leaving the information or content (television signal) itself out of its reach and under the Media Law.

(iv) It can be said that the changes aimed at unifying all network services under the same law are positive, ICT Law (previously television signal distribution networks were subject to the Media Law). Something similar can be said regarding the unification of the enforcement authority in the ENACOM.

(v) Decree 267/15 rationalizes many requirements included in the Media and ICT Laws, which generated a huge burden on providers and tended to unjustifiably complicate commercial traffic on provider companies and their licenses. In this sense, the simplification of the transfer and change of control regime as well as the transfer of licenses is seen as progress. Also noteworthy as an advance is the fact that the non-transferability of the television signal licenses has been repealed, as well as the flexibilization of the requirements for those who decide to provide the services regulated by both laws.

(vi) Introduced changes to the "transition regimen," dealing with different matters arising from the convergence between cable television market and telecommunications market which were legally separated. Cable television operators were authorized to enter the telecommunications market. Previously, telecommunication providers were forbidden to enter the cable television market.

(vii) It also appears positive that the rules for the accumulation of television signal licenses and coverage areas have been made more flexible. This flexibility was essential for broadcasters to be able to reach the "scale" necessary to find a sustainable business over time, which allows obtaining the economic resources to finance advanced services. We will see if it is sufficient, considering the absence of any basis on the matter.
The rigidity that the Media Law presented in this sense was highly criticized (and judicialized) and could, in the extreme, affect freedom of speech by making the provision of television signals commercially unsustainable due to the limitations it imposed.

(viii) However, the revision of the ICT Law and its confrontation with Decree 267/15 allows us to see that the National Executive limited itself to advancing on specific issues but that it has pending a task of enormous scope and importance for the future of the affected sectors, particularly that of the ICT Law, which continues to suffer from the necessary regulations to overcome the main criticism that this last law deserves, such as its serious level of abstraction and delegation to the National Executive.

(ix) Decree 267/15 initiated a complex drafting process in order to enact a unique law merging the current Media and ICT Laws. The proposed law that finally unifies the two regimes in question in a single legal body may be a propitious opportunity for some part of the governing normative principles in the matter to reach the hierarchy of law and not be just regulations to the law. This is to provide the sectoral regulations with greater predictability and stability in order to enable the heavy investments demanded by the sector. Within the framework of the analysis of the said project, it would be prudent to debate the reasonableness of submitting the content the television signals to the same law and enforcement authority that regulates and implements the legislation aimed at generating a competitive market for the development of the telecommunications infrastructure.

(x) Another aspect that deserves overcoming criticism is the independence of the authority for the application of the Media and ICT Laws, since ENACON is part of the National Administration, and its members are not endowed with any of the guarantees of an entity called to establish the regulatory policy of two sectors of such importance.

F. Recent Regulation Changes and New Amendments to the ICT Law

58. Among important changes in the regulation of media and telecommunication markets that followed the abovementioned Decree 264/15, it is worthy highlighting a few of them based upon the impact they produced in both markets:

- *ENACOM Resolution 1394/16* (Official Gazette April 22, 2016): Within the framework of what is established in Decree 267/15, ENACOM issued Resolution 1394/16 and approved a new General Regulation for the obtention of licenses to providing television signals distribution through physical and/ or radioelectric link, under the ICT Law.

  ENACOM Resolution 1394/16 conditions the provision of television services distribution under the ICT Law to be obtained by the provider: (i) of the Argentina Digital Single License, (ii) to the registration of the service in accordance with Article 5.4. of Annex I of Decree 764/2000, and (iii) the authorization of operation in at least one Coverage Area of the service in accordance with the provisions of the Regulations approved by the resolution.

  The resolution requires obtaining an operating authorization for each coverage area and the granting of the authorization requires the applicant to submit a copy of the ordinance or municipal resolution that authorizes the overhead or underground laying of the network, hindering technological convergence by hindering the direct use of networks, poles, columns, pipelines and existing infrastructure—own or third party. Applicants must submit for each area of coverage requested a Technical Draft in accordance with the current regulations, signed and validated by an engineer registered in the Professional Council of Telecommunications, Electronics and Computing Engineering (COPITEC—"Consejo Profesional de Ingeniería de Telecomunicaciones, Electrónica y Computación") or similar.

Meanwhile, those actors subject to the Media Law are free to enter the telecommunication market ruled by ICT Law without any additional requirement other than the license already granted under the ICT Law (i.e., authorization for each coverage area is not required).

The resolution does not admit the possibility that the applicant uses satellite facilities, a possibility that the providers excepted by Decree 267/15 and Res. ENACOM 1394/16; i.e., licensees under Media Law.

Regarding television signals to be distributed under the ICT Law, ENACOM's resolution set forth what is generally known as the "must-carry must-offer" rule of the following signals:

(i) the uncoded emission of the signals of "Radio Televisión Argentina Sociedad del Estado" (state-owned broadcaster); of all the stations and public signals of the National State and in all those in which the National State has participation;
(ii) the emission without coding of the signals of the Provincial States and the Autonomous City of Buenos Aires and the Argentine Catholic Church, whose coverage area coincides with the coverage area;
(iii) the inclusion, without coding, of the broadcasts of the original open (broadcasting) television license services whose coverage area coincides with the coverage area;
(iv) the inclusion of national news signals, individualized as such by ENACOM (as defined in Article 1 of ENACOM's resolution: signals which *"content is packaged and presents the news as thematic axis, including programming whose priority content is news, structuring them in various formats: news, journalistic, opinion tables, etc. relative to the events of the country in the different aspects of the socio-political and economic, cultural and sports order, both macro and micro (whether regional, provincial, local)."*).

– *Decree 1340/16* (Official Gazette January 2, 2017): Within the framework of what is established in Decrees 267/15, Decree 1340/16 implements standards to achieve a higher degree of convergence of networks and services under competitive conditions, promote the deployment of next-generation networks and the penetration of broadband internet access throughout the national territory, in accordance with the provisions of the Media and ICT Laws.

Despite being of a lower hierarchy than the ICT Law and Decree 267/15, this new Decree (standard, thus not equivalent to a formal law) aggravated the conditions for some companies in the telecommunications sector. Indeed, Decree

267/15 had recognized that in January 2018, the telecommunications service providers listed there could begin to provide the television signals distribution service (by physical or radio networks), but Decree 1340/16 established a new restriction provided that, as of January 1, 2018, these telecommunication operators could only provide said service in the cities of Buenos Aires and neighboring cities ("área mútible Buenos Aires" or "AMBA"), Rosario and Córdoba. On the contrary, the provision of the service in the rest of the cities of the country was conditioned *sine die* and at the sole discretion of ENACOM, without a specific waiting period having been established. Additionally, the television signal distribution service registration request submitted by the telecommunication companies affected by the temporary restrictions of Decree 267/15 to provide in AMBA cities and in the cities of Rosario and Córdoba could be delayed even more if an incumbent provider were to oppose to the new entrant.

Besides, Decree 1340/16 modified the restriction that existed under the ICT Law so that satellite television operators could offer telecommunications services but maintained the restriction so that telecommunications operators could not include satellite television in their convergent offer.

Decree 1340/16 also introduced a landmark change in the criteria behind ICT Law as amended by Decree 267/15, when it sets forth that for *"the term of 15 years, as from the enforcement of the Decree* [January 12th, 2017], *as a differentiated condition in the terms provided by article 45 of Law No. 27,078, for the protection of fixed last-mile NGN networks for broadband that deploy the licensees of Information Technology and Communications Services, regarding the rules of open access to broadband and infrastructure that are issued, without prejudice to the provisions of article 56 of the same Law."* Article 45 of the ICT Law *"… provides for the unbundling of the local network of ICT Services licensees. The Enforcement Authority will establish for this purpose the differentiated conditions based on technical, economic, opportunity, merit and convenience issues, attending to the preservation of the public interest and promoting competition."* while Article 56 of the same sets forth the "network-neutrality principle."

Accordingly, this simple decree repeals ICT Law as amended by Decree 267/15, suspending for fifteen years the "competition by services" in connection with the last mile, replacing it by the "competition by networks."

Regarding the entrance of the telecommunication licensees into television signal distribution, the decree also introduces major changes. While it maintains the entrance to AMBA, Rosario and Córdoba cities by January 1, 2018, for the rest of the country, the starting date for the provision of said service by the incumbent telecommunication licensees (included in Article 94, ICT Law, and detail above), will be determined by the ENACOM especially considering those localities with less than 80,000 inhabitants where the referred service is provided only by Cooperatives or Small and Medium businesses.

- *ENACOM Resolution 5160/17* (Official Gazette December 11, 2017): replaces the "must-offer and must-carry" obligation (set forth by ENACOM Resolution 1394/16 on April 22, 2016) for a "may-carry and may-offer" regimen.
- *ENACOM Resolution 5641/17* (Official Gazette December 22, 2017): in order to authorize the merger between the incumbent Telecom and Cablevisión-Fibertel

(television signal distribution operator who entered the telecommunication market by the end of the 1990s gaining important market shares across the country), which was incompatible with the "transition regimen" set forth by ICT Law and regulated by Decrees 267/15 and 1340/16, introduced the following changes:

(i) Extended until January 1, 2019, the starting term for the provision of the television signal distribution services (based both on physical and radioelectric link) by the incumbent telecommunication licensees (referred to in Article 94 of Law No. 27,078) in all those cities of the country—excluding the Autonomous City of Buenos Aires and neighboring cities in the Province of Buenos Aires; Rosario and Córdoba (Article 5, Decree 1340/16), which have less than 80,000 inhabitants, where the service is provided only by Cooperatives and Small and Medium Enterprises until January 1, 2019.

(ii) Established that in all those cities of the country—excluding the Autonomous City of Buenos Aires and neighboring cities in the Province of Buenos Aires; Rosario and Córdoba (Article 5, Decree 1340/16), whatever their number of inhabitants, where the television signal distribution services (based both on physical or radioelectric link) is provided by, at least, one licensee who has at the national level, a total number of subscribers greater than 700,000, the entry by the incumbent telecommunication licensees (referred to in Article 94 of Law No. 27,078) may occur as of January 1, 2018.

– *Necessity and Urgency Decree 690/20* (*Decreto de Necesidad y Urgencia* furnished with the same hierarchy of a law enacted from the National Congress—Official Gazette August 23, 2020): Implements strong and unforeseen changes in the policy towards the telecommunications sector resorting to the maximum level of economic regulation intervention recognized by Argentina National Constitution, legally declaring ICT services as public utilities, by virtue of which the relevant authority—ENACOM—is entitled to set tariffs and qualities and further regulate ICT services as public utility. Said decision coexists with economic regulation tools for the telecommunication markets globally accepted, such as the Universal Service regimen, aimed at assuring access to telecommunications services by those clients in the region which would not be able to pay prices freely set by the operators due to incomes restriction or geographics-demographics conditions determining costs that would be well above those registered in urban areas (ENACOM Resolution 2642/16—Official Gazette May 31, 2016).

Decree 690/20 amended the ICT Law, replacing several articles, among which are worth mentioning the following:

– Article 15 of ICT Law *"It is established that Information Technology and Communications (ICT) Services and access to telecommunications networks for and between licensees of ICT services are essential and strategic public services in competition. The enforcement authority will guarantee its effective availability."* ICT Law, as amended by Decree 267/15, only considered "public service" the latter, subject to interconnection usual terms and conditions.

- Article 48 of the ICT Law: *"The licensees of the Information and Communication Technologies (ICT) services will set their prices, which must be fair and reasonable, must cover the operating costs, tend towards efficient provision and a reasonable margin of operation. The prices of the essential and strategic public services of the ICT in competition, those provided in accordance with the Universal Service and those determined by the enforcement authority for reasons of public interest, will be regulated by it. The enforcement authority shall establish in the regulations the compulsory universal basic benefit that must be provided under equal conditions."*

  While ICT Law, as amended by Decree 267/15 (Article 48) and before it was amended by Decree 690/20, sets the freedom of the telecommunication licensees to establish the prices of their services and resort to the Universal Service regimen instead of providing for a *"compulsory universal basic benefit."*
- Article 54 of the ICT Law: "Incorporate as a public service, the mobile phone service in all its forms. The prices of these services will be regulated by the enforcement authority. The enforcement authority shall establish in the regulations the compulsory universal basic benefit that must be provided under equal conditions."

  Either ICT Law, as originally enacted and as amended by Decree 267/15, did not consider mobile phone service as a "public service" or set a "universal basic benefit." Based upon the new condition of "public service," Decree 690/20 suspends *" ... any price increase or modification thereof, established or announced from July 31 to December 31, 2020 by ICT licensees, including television signal distribution services through physical or radio link and those corresponding to telephone service fixed or mobile, in any of its modalities. This suspension will apply to subscription satellite television services."*

  While keeping the suspension abovementioned, ENACOM Resolution 1466/20 (Official Gazette December 21, 2020) authorized a 5% increase in the prices as of January 2021, considering a period in which national currency depreciation and inflation ratios were well above said percentage. Contemporaneously, ENACOM Resolution 1467/20 (Official Gazette December 21, 2020), in application of the "universal basic benefit" introduced by Decree 690/20, approved the "Mandatory Universal Basic Benefit" (*Prestación Básica Universal Obligatoria* (PBU)) which is mandatory for the incumbent telecommunication licensees—Telecom and Telefónica—mobile telecommunication licensees—Personal, Movistar and Claro—internet access providers—numberless of licensees—television signal distribution—again, numberless of licensees—and ICT services—also, numberless of licensees. In all cases, as of January 1, 2021.

  Additionally, in the cases of licensees of ICT and television signal distribution services with a "dominant position" in a given coverage area (those licensees holding more than 50% of the market in each area), the PBU must grant certain discounts (between 20% to 40% over the lower price plan by July 31, 2020, and following increase, depending on the number of subscribers). Thirteen categories of human beings and entities beneficiaries of a number of social programs are designated beneficiaries of the PBU; the precise number is quite difficult to determine in absence of a comprehensive database, but for sure reaches an important portion of the market. Moreover, the licensees cannot exclude a consumer from receiving the PBU without the previous approval of the ENACOM, aggravating the impact.

Rules regarding television signal mandatory and voluntarily distribution—ENACOM Resolution 1491/20 (Official Gazette December 24, 2020) approves a new Regulation for the television signal distribution service via physical, radio link and satellite networks (i.e., all technologies of television signal distribution), repealing all previous regulation on the subject matter, including ENACOM Resolution 1394/16 mentioned above. As mentioned above, this new regulation scope includes the television signal distribution via physical and radio link networks, governed by the ICT Law, as well as satellite networks, subject to the Media Law.

The licensees of the television signal distribution service via physical and radio link, ruled by ICT Law, must guarantee the distribution of the following television signals:

(i) the uncoded emission of the signals of "Radio Televisi6n Argentina Sociedad del Estado" (state-owned broadcaster); of all the stations and public signals of the National State and in all those in which the National State has participation;
(ii) the emission without coding of the signals of the Provincial States and the Autonomous City of Buenos Aires and of the Argentine Catholic Church, whose coverage area coincides with the coverage area;
(iii) the inclusion, without coding, of the broadcasts of the original open (broadcasting) television license services whose coverage area coincides with the coverage area;
(iv) the inclusion of those signals whose thematic axis is programming eminently federal informative, linked to regional, provincial spheres and local, in addition to the international and national informative content, as determined by the ENACOM.

59. In the case of the satellite television signal distribution service, subject to the Media Law, the obligation detail above is conditioned for technology reasons, in the following terms:

(i) public signs of the NATIONAL STATE and those in which it has participation, as well as those corresponding to the Provincial States, the City of Buenos Aires and the Argentine Catholic Church and the National Universities, in these last two cases, whose coverage area coincides with the up-link (uplink) of the television service systems Direct to Home ("Television Directa al Hogar");
(ii) the signals of origin corresponding to the licensee services of open television (broadcasting), whose coverage area coincides with the uplink of the systems of the Direct Home Television services;
(iii) four origin signals corresponding to the services of open television (broadcast) licensees whose coverage area does not coincide with the up-link of the

Direct Television services systems to home. This obligation will be free for television licensees to open television;

(iv) signs whose thematic axis is primarily federal informative programming, linked to the regional, provincial and local spheres, in addition to the international and national informative content, although they are not coincident with the up-link of the television services systems Direct to the Home and that are indicated by the ENACOM.

60. The inclusion of the signals detailed above will be subject to the conditions agreed between the parties. Its offer, free of charge, will generate the obligation of their inclusion by the licensees of the television signal distribution service either via physical, radio link or satellite networks. In those cases in which it is not possible to arrive at a fair and reasonable price for inclusion in the grid of a signal—mandatory or non-mandatory inclusion— any of the parties may request the intervention of the ENACOM, resorting to the dispute resolution proceeding set forth by ENACOM resolution 1194/20 (Official Gazette October 22, 2020). In absence of agreement, the signal shall be included in the programming grid at the price set by the ENACOM, based on the information collected in the procedure.

61. It is expressly forbidden to condition the assignment of one or several television signals to the acquisition of other signals. In case television signals package is offered, the price of each of them must be informed. In the event that there is no agreement between the parties, either of them may resort to the procedure described in the previous paragraph.

62. Finally, set forth the obligation of the television signal distribution subject to ENACOM resolution 1491/20 to include—within 180 administrative days (January 7, 2021)—at least one proprietary television signal, which shall be registered in the following thirty administrative days (February 22, 2021). Failure to comply with said obligation will be sanctioned according to the regime of sanctions in force for each type of service.

63. The intervention of the ICT Services market through Decree 690/20 is irreconcilable with the constitutional design of the Argentine Republic. The foundations of Decree 690/20 are insufficient to avoid its incompatibility with Articles 42 and 99, paragraph 3 of the National Constitution, among others.

64. The Argentine constitutional design in matters of economic regulation was updated in the last reform of the year 1994, reaffirming the presence of a model based on the private property of the means of production, the free market, and the defense of competition, as have Articles 9 to 12, 14, 17, 42 and related, of the National Constitution. In this constitutional scheme: *"The authorities will provide ... for the defence of competition against all forms of market distortion, for the control of natural and legal monopolies ... "* (Article 42—*"Las autoridades proveerán ... a la defensa de la competencia contra toda forma de distorsión de los mercados, al control de los monopolios naturales y legales ... "*). The justification for legal intervention in a market recognizes in our Constitution two hypotheses: the "distortion of the markets" and the presence of "monopolies." However, Decree 690/20 departs from these hypotheses.

65. Since the "digitization" of telecommunications networks and their "convergence" with the television signal distribution market (terrestrial and satellite), there has been a consensus at a global level that these markets do not have the status of "monopoly" and that they do not need to be classified as "public service" to meet the needs of the community.

66. This consensus is reflected, for example, in the studies and proposals for economic regulation for the ICT market proposed by the OECD, and, at the regional level, in the absence of a policy comparable to the one established by Decree 690/20, which generally does not regulate retail rates for ICT Services while dispute resolution mechanisms are envisaged at the wholesale level that may include the imposition of prices but only in the absence of agreement, precisely aiming to promote competition, while access to ICT Services is guaranteed through the so-called Universal Service regimes, regulatory intervention mechanisms that Argentina has had for decades, in order to ensure the affordability of ICT Services and competition as a guiding principle.

67. It is also paradoxical that the countries from which Argentina drew to develop the legal regime of "public service"—such as Spain and France—have gone beyond the traditional notion of this expression in the field of telecommunications to focus on ex ante regulation, in free private competition, in the control of wholesale prices to favor retail competition and, only as an exception, in the regulation of retail prices in situations of absence of effective competition.

68. In line with these backgrounds, the National Congress enacted in 2014 the ICT Law which classified ICT services as of "public interest" and reserved the classification of "public service in competition" for wholesale services, that is, for the contractual relations between the different operators among themselves, but not for the relations between the operators and their clients.

69. Instead, it seeks to regulate ICT services with the maximum intensity of state intervention possible, drastically modifying the industry rules established ex ante without any factual support to justify it. Thus, a situation of regulatory expropriation is presented that violates the principle of predictability and legal security, violates legal norms of a higher hierarchy, and goes against the international regulatory reality.

70. The Argentine Republic is bound by international agreements that it must respect. Within the framework of the World Trade Organization, Law 25,000 approved the fourth protocol annexed to the general agreement on trade in services in basic telecommunications, in which our country internationally committed not to impose limitations on access to the telecommunications market and make the terms and conditions of the licenses available to the public ex ante to provide the sector with a stable and predictable regulatory framework. As mentioned before, these legal norms have a higher hierarchy than national laws (National Constitution, Article 75, paragraph 22).

71. However, the fundaments expressed in the recitals of Decree 690/20 do not comply with the requirements of Article 42 of the National Constitution to justify the intervention of the ICT market under either of the two modalities described.

72. If by way of hypothesis a distortion was configured in any of the ICT markets, the National Executive Power should have reported it to the enforcement authority of the Law on Defence of Competition (which is integrated into the National Executive Power in the Secretariat of Commerce Interior, despite the fact that according to Law 27,442, Cap. IV, of May 2018, it should be an independent authority and with all the guarantees of impartiality).

73. There is no factual, technical, or legal basis that justifies the reasonableness of the declaration of ICT services as "public services" because there are multiple bidders who openly compete.

74. The obligation to guarantee the universality of the service with plans and prices differentiated according to the social interest has been in charge of the State since 2000 when a Trust Fund was established that has millionaire resources contributed by all private operators and that is administered by the control entity. It is, consequently, the State itself that has the duty and who has the resources to meet social needs that are not adequately satisfied by the market in free competition.

75. The decree has the nature of a decree of necessity and urgency, a norm of rank and legislative nature that the Constitution authorizes the National Executive Power to use exceptionally in the face of an emergency that must be solved immediately within a period incompatible with that required by the normal procedure of the laws.

76. Decree 690/20 does not allege, nor is it verified, the exceptional circumstances that prevent following the ordinary procedure for the sanction and promulgation of laws and that, therefore, enable the Executive Power to exercise the Legislative Power of the Nation that the Constitution assigned to the federal Congress.

77. Therefore, from this point of view, Decree 690/20 is unconstitutional, as it entails the usurpation of legislative functions.

78. With respect to the human right to access information, which Decree 690/20 claims to protect, its mere formulation presents problems. The right of access exists as such with respect to public information; regarding information in general, there is a right to seek, receive and disseminate information which must be protected from interference that may be generated by any type of monopoly, especially the one of the National State. Through this new decree, the income of ICT service providers is subjected to state control, which, far from ensuring their freedom and independence, makes them subject to all kinds of pressure from public officials on duty, in the case of ENACOM.

79. For all this, both our constituents and legislators established the terms of intervention in the markets, which were not complied with by Decree 690/20, resulting in their unconstitutionality. But they did not adopt these solutions in a capricious or dogmatic way, but they did so based on the knowledge of economic regulation, knowing that such constitutional and legal tools are the ones that allow maximizing the general welfare of the population, as well as any alternative solution that is available, should not only be dismissed as unconstitutional, but will lead to opposite results to the expansion in coverage, quality and affordability of ICT services (as a direct consequence of the lack of investments resulting from the legal and tariff uncertainty), and the breakdown of freedom of information, both by those who want to expose it to the rest of the public, and when they want to access it.

80. Decree 690/20 hits the very foundations of our organization—not only economic—but republican and democratic. Such a change in the rules of the game, in addition to affecting the acquired rights of the current operators in the ICT services market, will conspire against the arrival of new investments.

81. On April 30, 2021, the Administrative Court of Appeals admitted the injunction requested by Telecom Argentina S.A. (hereinafter referred to as "Telecom") in the lawsuit "TELECOM ARGENTINA S.A. c/ EN-ENACOM Y OTRO s/MEDIDA CAUTELAR (AUTONOMA)" (File No. 12881/2020), and therefore ordered the suspension of the legal enforcement of Articles 1, 2, 3, 4, 5 and 6 of the Decree 690/20, and of ENACOM's Resolutions Nos. 1466/2020, 1467/2020 and 204/2021 (hereinafter referred to as "Resolutions 1466/20, 1467/20 and 204/21"), only as applicable to Telecom.

82. Telecom brought a lawsuit against the National Executive Branch and the ENACOM, requesting an injunction to suspend the legal enforcement of Decree 690/20 and of Resolutions 1466/20 and 1467/20. Telecom argued that these regulations had violated Articles 14, 17, 19, 28, 31, 32, 33, 42, 75, subsections 22, 76 and 99, subsection 3 of the National Constitution, as well as the provisions of Article 30 of the American Convention on Human Rights (ACHR).

83. The Administrative Court of Appeals considered that, through Decree 690/20, the National Executive Branch had introduced permanent modifications in Law No. 27,078 (Ley de Argentina Digital), granting to all ICT Services and access to telecommunications networks for and between the licensees of ICT and mobile phone services, the nature of "public utilities services in competition." It was also considered that the DNU 690/20 had established a series of regulations that would likely affect substantially the conditions of services provision and that price and fare regulations imposed by the government would have a negative impact on the plaintiff's income.

84. In conclusion, the Appellate Court granted Telecom's appeal and overruled the decision of the Trial Court and, consequently, ordered the suspension of the legal enforcement effects of Articles 1, 2, 3, 4, 5 and 6 of Decree 690/2020 and Resolutions 1466/2020, 1467/2020 and 204/21. Therefore, it was ruled that none of those regulations would be applicable to Telecom for a six-month period.

85. Other telecommunications licensees (and an association representing them) obtained similar precautionary measures.

G. Recent Antitrust Ruling Regarding Worldwide Disney: Fox Economic Concentration

86. The Resolution of the Secretary of Domestic Trade No. 11, of January 17, 2022 ("Resolution"), following the terms of Ruling of the National Commission for the Defense of Competition (hereinafter, "CNDC"), which is part of the resolution in comment, issued on the economic concentration operation consisting of the acquisition of exclusive control by the Walt Disney Company (hereinafter, "DISNEY") on TWENTY-FIRST CENTURY FOX, INC. (hereinafter "FOX"). The acquisition included FOX's TV and movie studios, cable entertainment networks and international TV business. The operation in question is of a global nature and, therefore, has effects in the Argentine Republic. As reported by the parties, the closing date of the transaction was March 20, 2019.

87. The Resolution provides:

(i) The operation as notified on March 19, 2019 is affected by the prohibition of Article 8 of the Law for the Defense of Competition 27,442—"LDC"—by establishing or strengthening a position of dominance in the production and marketing of signals.
(ii) Rejects the commitments offered by the parties by virtue of having concluded that they do not reverse the anticompetitive effects of the operation, which led the authority to consider it framed in the aforementioned prohibition.
(iii) For this reason, it subordinates the approval of the operation to the fulfillment of a series of structural conditions, the realization of which will necessarily take time, for which it adds certain behavioral conditions in order to ensure—in both cases—that the main sporting events that identified as fundamental are distributed by a new vigorous actor independent of the parties to the transaction.
(iv) Delegates to the CNDC the monitoring of compliance with the conditions, which may request the information it deems necessary for this purpose, as well as, upon well-founded request of the parties, recommend to the Secretary of Domestic Trade to grant an extension of terms for compliance with the established conditions or provide for their exemption or modification.
(v) Considers the opinion of the CNDC as an integral part of the Resolution.

88. Among the arguments upon which the decision was adopted, it can be highlighted that in the view of the antitrust authority, the concentration operation under analysis would eliminate a relevant competitor in the sports signals market since ESPN and FOX SPORTS signals are the closest competitors in said market.

89. Likewise, the aforementioned bundling could prevent or delay the emergence in Argentina of new operators and/or new forms of commercialization of pay television signals, such as the skinny bundle, streaming services, OTT, etc., preventing or delaying competition and innovation in the pay television market.

90. Consequently, the economic concentration operation in question has the potential to restrict or distort competition in such a way that it may be detrimental to the general economic interest in relation to the market for pay television sports signals.

91. The CNDC considered that the remedies offered by the parties, although they acknowledge the existence of a market problem, are not sufficient to mitigate the aforementioned horizontal and conglomerate effects.

92. Accordingly, the CNDC preferred the application of a structural-type remedial measure rather than a behavioral-type remedy, since its effects are long-lasting, directly attacking the source of the competitive damage at its root and tending to eliminate the circumstances that originated it (e.g., market power) while creating new competitors or strengthening existing ones. This structural remedy can be complemented with behavioral remedial measures.

93. Therefore, it rejects the conditions offered by the notifiers and conditions the operation to the following requirements (conf. Article 14, LDC):

Structural measures:

i. within 12 months of notification of the resolution (dated 01/17/2022), plus an extension of 6 months. transfer of all transmission rights related to sports tournaments and competitions of which FOX SPORTS was the licensor at the time of notification of the operation (and that currently remain in the possession of the Parties) for local and exclusive transmission to a Sub-Licensee approved by this CNDC, to a new vigorous competitor in the sports signals market of the basic pay TV grid;
ii. the divestment process will be considered completed in the case of transferring, at least, the main sports content of each of the sports, classified as follows: (i) Soccer championships where teams from the first division of the Professional League participate of the Argentine Soccer; (ii) International soccer leagues or tournaments where teams from the first division of the Argentine Professional Soccer League do not participate; (iii) American Football; (iv) Baseball; (v) Motorsports; (vi) Fight; (vii) Wrestling; (viii) Boxing; (ix) Basketball; (x) Rugby; and (xi) Tennis;

iii. to renew the television rights of the sporting events subject to divestment with the international licensor, they must provide for the sublicense for Argentina;
iv. from the Resolution and until the effective transfer, they must keep the existing signals and programming, guaranteeing the transmission of all the events over which they have rights;
v. once the transfer has been made or the 18-month term imposed for it has expired, they must reduce the basic sports linear signals offered in Argentina from 7 to 4.
vi. prior to this, they must provide an open and free transmission plan for the contents that are excluded as a result of such a reduction in signals.

Behavioral measures: once the 18-month period has elapsed without the transfer having been completed, you will have to comply with the following behaviors, for 5 years:

i. extend the rights over the signals pre-existing to the operation;
ii. offer the signals without packaging or commercial discounts for joint contracting or obligation to transmit non-contracted signals;
iii. eliminate from these contracts, minimum resale prices, number of subscribers, percentages of penetration and number of subscribers;
iv. require that the cost of premium sports signals must not exceed the income of cable operators for that content;
v. have a maximum of 4 linear sports signals in the grid offered in Argentina;
vi. they will not be able to transmit the events subject to divestment and, if acquired, they must sublicense them for their exclusive transmission in Argentina.

Additional behavioral measures:

1. make available to open and pay TV signals that so require, the relevant events of each of the competencies subject to divestment:
   a. after the disinvestment period has expired, this will be limited to events that were not disinvested;
   b. such retransmission will be free;
   c. the events will be defined by the SCI, prior opinion of the CNDC, at the proposal of the parties.
2. make available to the open and pay TV signals that so require, two relevant matches of the Argentine Professional Soccer League, one of which must include Boca or River, a requirement that will be in force as long as the divestment does not reach the "Soccer Championships where the first division team of the Argentine Professional Soccer League participates";
3. the events will be defined by the SCI, prior opinion of the CNDC, at the proposal of the parties;

4. The cost of the sports signals of the parties to the operation may not exceed the maximum percentage of the basic subscription registered before the notification of the operation.

Exclusive Sublicense Agreements:

i. the parties to the operation may not transmit the events reached, for a period of 5 years;
ii. the term of the contract must be at least 5 years;
iii. shall not:
    1. limit the competitive capacity of the sub-licensee, including its advertising or sales strategy;
    2. establish consideration in favor of the parties to the operation based on the performance of the sub-licensee;
    3. allow the parties to the operation access to sensitive competitive information of the sub-licensee;
    4. include grounds for termination not included in the license agreement;
    5. approval of the SCI, prior opinion of the CNDC, verifying the independence and capacity of the sub-licensee, who may not have any corporate relationship with the parties to the operation.

H. Recent Antitrust Ruling: Incumbent Telecom and Artear Sanctioned for Abusing Their Dominant Position in the Pay TV Market

94. Telecom imposed discriminatory sales conditions on another pay TV operator for the signals Canal 13[15] (prevailing broadcasting signal) and TN[16] (prevailing news signal distributed via cable), both owned by the company ARTEAR and belonging to the same economic group (Grupo Clarín), preventing its entry and development as a competitor in the pay TV market and restricting its ability to competitively replicate the quadruple play service. The sanction consists of a fine of ARS 150 million.[17]

95. The investigation began as a result of a complaint filed by Claro Argentina, an American Móvil that operates in Argentina and provides mobile and fixed telephone services, internet services and pay TV services. According to the complaint, Grupo Clarín imposed on Claro Argentina sales conditions for the signals Canal 13

15. https://www.eltrecetv.com.ar/?gclid=CjwKCAjwitShBhA6EiwAq3RqA-4NRg3JMdVrAqudN4tktaQ2C_qkjAPNxkvv-jo0R63iRl31i7carRoCQIEQAvD_BwE.
16. https://tn.com.ar/?gclid=CjwKCAjwitShBhA6EiwAq3RqA8PtNjpLM2P2oGDXbf8C-BYqODmwOuCtsK92u59l3umvSVj4gGZPAxoCTaoQAvD_BwE.
17. *See* https://www.argentina.gob.ar/defensadelacompetencia/telecom-and-artear-sanctioned-abusing-their-dominant-position-pay-tv-market.

and TN that prevented its acquisition, hindering its entry as a pay TV operator in the geographic markets of the AMBA and the cities of Córdoba and Rosario, by the way of restricting its ability to competitively replicate the quadruple play service.

96. Telecom is the leading telecommunications company in Argentina, with a nationwide presence. As a result of the merger between Grupo Clarín and Telecom, it became the first and only company to offer quadruple play (mobile telephony, fixed telephony, Internet and pay TV), with a predominant market share in different regions of the country. In turn, Grupo Clarín, through the firm ARTEAR, is engaged in the production of television content and signals, specifically Canal 13, TN, Volver, Metro, Canal A, Quiero Música and Magazine.

97. The investigation corroborated that ARTEAR has a dominant position in the air channels segment, with the signal Canal 13, and in the pay television channels, with the news content segment, with the signal TN. Likewise, it was verified that in the pay TV service markets of AMBA, Córdoba city and Rosario city, Telecom has a dominant position with a share of more than 50% of the subscribers, while Claro is an entrant in such markets, with a share of less than 1%.

98. In effect, the CNDC found evidence of the commission of an abuse of dominant position by the firms Artear and Telecom in the urban agglomerations of AMBA, the city of Córdoba and the city of Rosario, from December 2017 to July 2021, consisting in the imposition of discriminatory conditions for the acquisition of transmission rights of their television signals to AMX (Claro), by discretionary fixing minimum subscriber amounts, and as a consequence hindering and obstructing AMX's entry to the pay TV market.

99. The conduct generated damage to competition in the aforementioned pay TV markets and caused harm to the general economic interest, inasmuch as the denounced companies generated an artificial barrier to enter the pay TV markets in the geographic areas where Telecom operates or has plans to do so, obstructing the entry of AMX and/or other potential competitors, by means of the requirement of Artear—holder of the rights over two of the highest rated signals of Argentine television—of minimum subscriber ramps impossible to be met by an entrant firm. Faced with this imposition, AMX, like any other new entrant operator, found itself in the position of having to choose between not including those signals in its grid and offering a lower quality product or including them and selling its subscription at a higher price than that of its competitor (Telecom).

100. In turn, by establishing artificial barriers to the entry of new players and restricting the ability of new entrants to compete, Telecom maintained its dominant position in the pay TV market, which has allowed it to obtain a supracompetitive benefit in the quadruple play service, which is detrimental to consumers.

101. The Argentina Defence of Competition Law, Law No. 27,442, in its section 3, specifies that certain commercial practices, when carried out by a human or legal person with a dominant position in a market, maybe framed as anticompetitive conduct. For instance, when those practices: (a) prevent, hinder or obstruct third parties from entering or remaining in a market or exclude them from it, and/or (b) impose discriminatory conditions for the acquisition or alienation of goods or services without reasons based on commercial uses and customs. As established in section 1 of the mentioned act, these practices are prohibited and subject to penalties.

§3. Sources of Media Law

102. As referred to above, the original Argentine Constitution was enacted in 1853 and amended on several occasions, the last of which was in 1994. Chapter I of Part I of the Constitution establishes a bill of rights for all individuals, Argentinean or foreign, which includes the recognition and protection of life, work, commerce, liberty, equality, security, and property, publishing their ideas in the press without prior censorship, among others.

103. Section 32 expressly sets forth: "The Federal Congress shall not pass laws that restrict freedom of the press or establish federal jurisdiction over it."

104. According to the Constitution, International treaties have the same hierarchy as the Constitution itself or as laws enacted by Congress. According to sections 31 and 75 (paragraph 22) of the Argentine Constitution, international treaties, once approved by Congress and ratified by the government, take precedence over federal and provincial laws.

105. The international treaties with constitutional hierarchy related to freedom of thought and speech entered into by Argentina are:

- American Declaration of Human Rights and Obligations (Declación Americana de los Derechos y Deberes del Hombre), agreed in the IX American International Conference, Bogotá, Colombia, 1948, which Article IV states: *"Every human being has the right to freedom of investigation, of opinion and of expression and dissemination of thought by any means."*
- Universal Declaration of Human Rights (Declaración Universal de Derechos Humanos), approved by Resolution 217(III) of the General Assembly of the United Nations on December 10, 1948, which Article 19 states: *"Every human being has the right to freedom of opinion and expression; this right includes the right not to be disturbed because of their opinions, to investigate and receive information and opinions, and to disseminate them, without limitation of borders, by any means of expression."*
- International Convention of Human Rights agreed as part of the San José de Costa Rica Treaty (Pacto de San José de Costa Rica sobre Convención Americana de Derechos Humanos), signed on November 22, 1984, and approved by Argentina law 23,054 (Official Gazette March 27, 1984) which Article 13 sets forth the freedom of thought and speech.

– International Treaties of Economic, Social, Cultural right, Civil rights and Political rights approved by Resolution 2200(XXI) of the General Assembly of the United Nations and approved by Argentina law 23,313 (Official Gazette May 13, 1986) which Article 19 sets forth the freedom of thought and speech.

106. The National Executive Power is entitled to promote and defense of the national audiovisual industry within the framework of the provisions of Article 75, subsection 19 of the National Constitution. To this end, it must adopt measures aimed at promoting the formation and development of national audiovisual content production conglomerates for all formats and supports, facilitating dialogue, cooperation and business organization between economic actors and public, private, and public institutions and academic, for the benefit of competitiveness (section 153, Media Law).

107. For this, frameworks will be established that aim to:

(a) Train the sectors involved on the importance of creating value in the area not only in its industrial aspect but also as a mechanism for promoting cultural diversity and its expressions.
(b) Promote the development of the activity with a federal orientation, which considers and stimulates the local production of the provinces and regions of the country.
(c) Promote the activity of producers who start in the activity.
(d) Develop lines of action aimed at strengthening the sustainable development of the audiovisual sector.
(e) Implement measures aimed at identifying businesses and markets for the insertion of audiovisual production abroad.
(f) Facilitate access to information, technology and existing institutional settings for this purpose.
(g) Develop strategies and international co-productions that allow the production of more television and radio of an educational, cultural and children's nature. To this end, it must provide for the creation of a Competitive Development Fund for the Production of Quality Television Programs for Boys, Girls and Adolescents (section 153, Media Law).

Part I. Freedom of Speech

108. Over the last three decades, Argentina has developed important protections for freedom of expression through the jurisprudence of the Supreme Court. Thus, case law has developed relevant doctrines that, for example, distinguish between private and public individuals, as well as between public and private interests, and protect journalists and the general public from criminal and tort liability for defamation when it comes to information of public interest.

109. However, most of the protections are based on case law rather than specific legislation. In some cases, that may involve certain contingencies, considering that Supreme Court decisions are not binding on cases other than the one decided and (although highly persuasive) are not binding on lower courts.

§1. Legal Framework of the Right to Freedom of Expression

110. Freedom of speech and expression is recognized and protected under Argentine laws. Article 14 of Argentina's National Constitution establishes the right to publish ideas without prior censorship[18] and Article 32 prohibits Congress from passing laws limiting press freedom.[19] Finally, with the Constitutional reform of 1994, international human rights treaties, including the ACHR, acquired constitutional hierarchy under Article 75, paragraph 22.[20]

---

18. Argentine Constitution, Art. 14: "*All inhabitants of the Nation enjoy the following rights in accordance with the laws regulating their exercise, namely: to work and exercise all lawful industries; to navigate and trade; to petition the authorities; to enter, stay, transit and leave Argentine territory; to publish their ideas in the press without prior censorship; to use and dispose of their property; to associate for useful purposes; to freely profess their religion; to teach and learn*" ("*Todos los habitantes de la Nación gozan de los siguientes derechos conforme a las leyes que reglamenten su ejercicio; a saber: de trabajar y ejercer toda industria lícita; de navegar y comerciar; de peticionar a las autoridades; de entrar, permanecer, transitar y salir del territorio argentino; de publicar sus ideas por la prensa sin censura previa; de usar y disponer de su propiedad; de asociarse con fines útiles; de profesar libremente su culto; de enseñar y aprender.*").
19. Argentine Constitution, Art. 32: "*The federal Congress shall make no law abridging the freedom of the press or establishing federal jurisdiction over it*" ("*El Congreso federal no dictará leyes que restrinjan la libertad de imprenta o establezcan sobre ella la jurisdicción federal.*").
20. Argentine Constitution, Art. 75, inciso 22: "*It is incumbent upon Congress: (...) [t]o test or reject treaties concluded with other nations and with international organizations and concordats with the Holy See. Treaties and concordats have hierarchy superior to laws. The American Declaration of the Rights and Duties of Man; the Universal Declaration of Human Rights; the American Convention on Human Rights; the International Covenant on Economic, Social and Cultural Rights; the*

111. Argentina's Penal Code, however,, criminalizes defamation but excludes nonassertive expressions and expressions related to public interest from liability.[21] The Penal Code describes a number of crimes related to freedom of expression.[22] The chapter on crimes against the public order provides for the crime of public intimidation, penalizing with two to six years of imprisonment anyone who, in order to spread general fear or cause a riot or disorder, makes any sign, sounds an alarm, threatens to commit any crime of common danger, or uses any other physical means that would normally produce any such result. This penalty is increased to imprisonment for three to ten years if explosives or chemical substances were used in the perpetration of the crime.

112. Anyone who publicly incites collective violence against groups of persons or institutions is sanctioned with imprisonment for three to six years for the incitement alone.

International Covenant on Civil and Political Rights and its Optional Protocol; the Convention on the Prevention and Punishment of the Crime of Genocide; the International Convention on the Elimination of All Forms of Racial Discrimination; the Convention on the Elimination of All Forms of Discrimination against Women; the Convention against Torture and Other Cruel, Inhuman or Degrading Treatment or Punishment; the Convention on the Rights of the Child; under the conditions of their validity, have constitutional hierarchy, do not derogate from any article of the first part of this Constitution and must be understood as complementary to the rights and guarantees recognized therein. They may only be denounced, as the case may be, by the National Executive Power, with the prior approval of two thirds of the totality of the members of each House. Other treaties and conventions on human rights, after being approved by the Congress, shall require the vote of two thirds of the totality of the members of each Chamber to enjoy constitutional hierarchy" ("*Corresponde al Congreso: (...) [a]probar o desechar tratados concluidos con las demás naciones y con las organizaciones internacionales y los concordatos con la Santa Sede. Los tratados y concordatos tienen jerarquía superior a las leyes. La Declaración Americana de los Derechos y Deberes del Hombre; la Declaración Universal de Derechos Humanos; la Convención Americana sobre Derechos Humanos; el Pacto Internacional de Derechos Económicos, Sociales y Culturales; el Pacto Internacional de Derechos Civiles y Políticos y su Protocolo Facultativo; la Convención sobre la Prevención y la Sanción del Delito de Genocidio; la Convención Internacional sobre la Eliminación de todas las Formas de Discriminación Racial; la Convención sobre la Eliminación de todas las Formas de Discriminación contra la Mujer; la Convención contra la Tortura y otros Tratos o Penas Crueles, Inhumanos o Degradantes; la Convención sobre los Derechos del Niño; en las condiciones de su vigencia, tienen jerarquía constitucional, no derogan artículo alguno de la primera parte de esta Constitución y deben entenderse complementarios de los derechos y garantías por ella reconocidos. Sólo podrán ser denunciados, en su caso, por el Poder Ejecutivo nacional, previa aprobación de las dos terceras partes de la totalidad de los miembros de cada Cámara. Los demás tratados y convenciones sobre derechos humanos, luego de ser aprobados por el Congreso, requerirán del voto de las dos terceras partes de la totalidad de los miembros de cada Cámara para gozar de la jerarquía constitucional.*").

21. *See* E. Bertoni y A. Del Campo, Calumnias e Injurias, A dos Años de la Reforma del Codigo Penal Argentino, CELE, September 2012, available at http://www.palermo.edu/cele/pdf/Calumnias-e-Injurias.pdf for a discussion on the history, application and effectiveness of the law that decriminalized public interest speech in 2009.
22. Código Penal de la República Argentina [Cód. Pen.] [Penal Code], Ley 11.179, B.O., Nov. 3, 1921 (revised 1984), http://servicios.infoleg.gob.ar/infolegInternet/anexos/15000-19999/16546/texact.htm #22.

113. In addition, the Penal Code contains an entire chapter on the protection of the right to honor. It sanctions with a fine of ARS 3,000 to 30,000 anyone who slanders or falsely accuses another of a crime. Anyone who intentionally dishonors or discredits another is subject to a fine of ARS 1,500 to 20,000. However, the sanction does not apply to expressions concerning matters of public interest or those that are not assertive.

§2. Limitations of Freedom of Expression

114. The constitutional right to freedom of expression is not an absolute right and, according to Supreme Court decisions, may be limited if:

(1) it is established by law;
(2) it has a legal purpose; and
(3) it meets the needs of a democratic society and is proportionate to that need.[23]

115. In addition, the Supreme Court has unequivocally established that limitations on freedom of expression must always be interpreted restrictively.[24]

§3. Jurisprudence

116. Argentina's Supreme Court has developed an extensive jurisprudence on freedom of expression throughout its history. The Court has in fact recognized the necessary link between freedom of speech and democracy and has quoted and cited international and regional jurisprudence and standards in its decisions.

117. The Court has traditionally distinguished public and private interests, as well as public and private figures, to afford wider protections for expression referring to public matters. This distinction was made and upheld jurisprudentially even prior to the legislative reform that led to the decriminalization of public interest speech and nonassertive expression in 2009.[25] Similarly, the Court upheld the doctrine of actual malice in cases dealing with defamation of public officials and developed protections for the reproduction of third-party expressions through the Campillay doctrine.[26]

---

23. Centro de Estudios en Libertad de Expresión y Acceso a la Información, Tendencias en la Libertad de Expresión en Argentina 3 (March 2018), https://www.palermo.edu/cele/pdf/Libertad_de_expresi on_en_Argentina.pdf.
24. Anecdotally, it may be worth noting that disruption of speeches by hecklers is not uncommon in Argentina. A recent example occurred at an event held by the head of the National Library at which the speaker was disrupted by protests while he was speaking; the protesters were removed from the room by security guards but apparently not arrested.
25. *See Id.* Also *See*, CSJN, Patitó, José Angel y otro c/ Diario La Nación y otros, Fallos: 331:1530.
26. *See*, Supreme Court, Campillay, Julio César c/La Razón y otros, Fallos: 308:789.

I. *Sujarchuck v. Warley*[27]

118. Argentina does not have specific laws governing liability for online intermediaries for third party posted content. In the absence of such laws, the jurisprudence of the Supreme Court, although not binding on other cases, acquires particular relevance.

119. The case involves Mr Sujarchuk and Mr Warley, two public officials at the School of Communications at Universidad de Buenos Aires (UBA). Upon Mr Sujarchuk's designation, Mr Marcos Britos wrote an article entitled "News regarding the presence of Ariel Sujarchuk at UBA," criticizing his past performance, alleged dark businesses and reputation. Mr Warley posted the article to his blog "Desde el aula" and added the word "Sinister" to the title, thus reading: "News regarding the presence of "sinister" Ariel Sujarchuck at UBA." Mr Sujarchuk thereafter initiated a tort claim for defamation against Mr Warley arguing that hosting the article and changing the title constituted endorsements of the defamatory character of the article written by Mr Britos.

120. The Supreme Court on its decision of August 2013 adopted the Attorney General's (AG's) opinion in its entirety, holding that there were no grounds for liability against Mr Warley. In doing so, the AG used a standard developed in the 1980s known as the Campillay doctrine, establishing that a person cannot be liable for the reproduction of information as long as there is clear attribution to the source and the contents are not substantially altered. The AG understood that adding the word "sinister" to the title did not substantially alter the content of the article drafted and clearly attributed to Mr Britos. The Sujarchuk case marks the first case where the Supreme Court reviewed the liability of intermediaries for third-party content posted to a blog. The case provides an insight into the AG and the Supreme Court's rationale for future decisions where the intermediaries are not bloggers but important search engines (i.e., Google and Yahoo). Several cases are in the pipeline and on their way to the Supreme Court dealing with this same issue and particular attention should be paid to what the Court decides then.[28]

II. *Canicoba Corral v. Acevedo*[29]

121. The case of *Canicoba Corral v. Acevedo* came only two weeks after the *Sujarchuk v. Warley* case, on August 14, 2013. In this case, the Court went into a substantial review of defamation law and the decision, unlike Sujarchuk, constitutes a major setback in freedom of expression jurisprudence. Mr Canicoba Corral was a federal judge appointed during the mandate of President C. Menem in the 1990s.

27. *See,* Supreme Court, Ariel Bernardo c/Warley, Jorge A. s/daños y perjuicios, Fallos, S.755.XLVI., 01/08/13.
28. *See* for example, Da Cunha Virginia c/Yahoo de Argentina SRL y Otros/daños y perjuicios—S.C., D.544, L.XLVI.
29. *See* Supreme Court, Canicoba Corral, Rodolfo Arístides c/Acevedo, Sergio Edgardo y otros s/daños y perjuicios, Fallos: C. 1079; XLV, 14/08/13.

Mr Acevedo was a former governor of Santa Cruz and former Chair of the Impeachment Committee in the House of Representatives. In a media interview, Mr Acevedo stated that Mr Canicoba Corral, along with other judges appointed during the same presidential mandate, was "despicable" ("detestable"). Judge Canicoba Corral launched a civil lawsuit for defamation.

122. The Supreme Court in a divided decision ruled in favor of the plaintiff. After following the traditional review in freedom of speech cases, distinguishing between public officials and private individuals, public interest and public duties, the Supreme Court concluded that in this case, Mr Acevedo's comments exceeded reasonable criticism and constituted an insult that affected Mr Canicoba Corral's professional reputation. The insult was heightened according to the Court in light of Mr Acevedo's prior positions as a public figure. This marks the first case where the Court upheld a decision against criticism involving a public figure in exercise of his/her duties.

123. The Supreme Court had said in prior cases that the right to free speech did not create a right to insult but had never upheld a decision on liability based on this argument.[30] The decision in this case rejects the distinction between assertive and nonassertive expression as the basis for liability and lays a dangerous foundation for future defamation cases. Limitations on the right to criticize the judiciary and its members need to be restrictively interpreted. These and other arguments along these lines were the basis for the petition launched by Mr Acevedo against Argentina in the Inter-American Commission on Human Rights (IACHR) in January 2014.[31]

III. *Grupo Clarin SA v. National State*

124. Very few Supreme Court cases have sparked such intense debate among ordinary citizens as the *Grupo Clarin S.A. v. National State case*. This case was argued in the social, cultural, and legal contexts simultaneously. And it gave rise to such polarization among scholars, professionals, and the overall population that the decision itself was overshadowed by expectations.

125. In 2009, the Argentine Congress passed Law 26,522, known as the media law. Article 45 sets a cap on the number of radio frequencies and TV licenses any one company or person can own. Per Article 161, any company who at the time of the enactment of the law exceeded the number of permitted licenses had a one-year period to sell, divide or reformulate their companies to comply with the regulation. Grupo Clarin SA was among the companies that exceeded the number of permitted licenses and questioned the constitutionality of the law on several grounds. The

30. *See* Supreme Court, Patitó, José Angel y otro c/Diario La Nación y otros, Fallos: 331:1530.
31. *See* that petition in https://www.cels.org.ar/common/documentos/PETICION%20%20FINAL%20Denuncia%20Acevedo.pdf.

most important point for this paper is that reducing their structure could compromise the profitability of the company and force it to close, therefore creating an indirect restriction on freedom of expression.

126. The Supreme Court issued its decision in October 2013, holding that the media law was constitutional. The Court first addressed the importance of freedom of expression and the press in a democratic society. It then evaluated the State's means to protect freedom of speech and expression in its social and individual dimensions and finally reviewed the constitutionality of the law in light of the interests being balanced. The decision held that freedom of expression in its social dimension is necessary to guarantee freedom of information and the development of public opinion. Unlike the individual dimension of free speech, the Court said, guaranteeing the social dimension of this right requires the State's active involvement and participation.[32] Therefore, the Court stated that the State has an unquestionable interest in regulating mass media, as it is through mass media that freedom of expression is materialized.[33]

127. Having established the duty of the State to intervene (a priori through regulation or a posteriori through sanctions) in order to protect free speech in its social dimension, the Court moved to evaluate whether the law constituted an indirect restriction to freedom of expression in the particular case. Plaintiffs had argued that the cap on the number of licenses jeopardized the economic sustainability of the company, thus constituting an indirect restriction to freedom of expression.

128. The Supreme Court held that unlike the leading case *Editorial Rio Negro v. Neuquén* (2007),[34] dealing with discrimination in the attribution of public advertising, in this case, there was, a priori, no differentiated treatment against the plaintiff that could justify shifting the burden of proof against the constitutionality of the law. It then concluded that based on the evidence provided in the case (including expert witnesses), implementing the law would not impair the economic sustainability of the group to constitute an indirect restriction.

129. Finally, the Supreme Court reviewed the constitutionality of the law balancing the right to ownership and property alleged by the plaintiff against the right to freedom of expression in its social dimension as alleged by the State. The decision upheld the constitutionality of the law applying a non-strict level of scrutiny, concluding that the alleged restriction was reasonable and proportionate to the need to regulate social media in a democratic society. The Court did not evaluate the necessity of such law, nor did it enter into its efficiency or effectiveness in achieving its declared purpose. Instead, it deferred to Congress, recognizing them with a wide margin of appreciation in this regard.

32. *See* Supreme Court, Grupo Clarín SA y otros c/Poder Ejecutivo Nacional y otros/acción meramente declarativa, Fallos, G. 439. XLIX. (REX); G. 445. XLIX.; G. 451. XLIX, Considerando 25.
33. *See* Supreme Court, Grupo Clarín SA y otros c/Poder Ejecutivo Nacional y otros/acción meramente de *See* clarativa, Fallos, G. 439. XLIX. (REX); G. 445. XLIX.; G. 451. XLIX, Considerando 23.
34. Supreme Court, Grupo Clarín SA y otros c/Poder Ejecutivo Nacional y otros/acción meramente declarativa, Fallos, G. 439. XLIX. (REX); G. 445. XLIX.; G. 451. XLIX, Considerando 23.

130. The decision in *Grupo Clarin S.A. v. National State* developed the social dimension of the right to freedom of expression. Although the Court had cited this aspect of freedom of speech in prior cases, the analysis always pivoted around the individual dimension of this important right. Interestingly, the Court avoided the contrast between the individual and social dimensions of freedom of speech and took a different approach, confronting economic rights against freedom of speech instead. Furthermore, the decision raised a number of issues that could lead to further litigation. The Court stated that the Constitutionality of the law rested upon its purpose—i.e., the promotion of the social dimension of freedom of expression—and that said purpose could be trumped: (1) by discriminatory use of government advertising; (2) by not guaranteeing an independent control authority.

IV. *Artear v. National State*[35]

131. The case of Artear does not bring novel issues on freedom of speech to the Supreme Court for review. Instead, it brings an old issue that remains unsolved: the issue of government advertising and the lack of objective and transparent criteria to distribute it. The decision, however, is important for its analysis of the value and force of the Court's own precedents and decisions and the importance of state compliance with judicial orders to uphold the rule of law.

132. Artear dealt with government advertising as an indirect restriction to freedom of expression. The plaintiff filed a complaint stating that the distribution of government advertising was discriminatory and discretional. They also stated that their quota for government advertising had been limited and reduced to virtually non-existent in an attempt to control their editorial content.

133. The Supreme Court on its decision of February 2014 referred the issue of government advertising entirely to Editorial Rio Negro as the leading case in this area. Instead of re-addressing the freedom of speech issue, the decision was centered around the value of prior Supreme Court decisions on other branches of government as well as lower courts and the dangers created by the Executive's noncompliance with judicial decisions.

134. The cases of Editorial Rio Negro[36] and Editorial Perfil[37] are examples of the Executive's utter disregard for judicial decisions. In both cases, the Court ordered the State to eliminate discriminatory practices in the distribution of government advertising and even gave the State a peremptory timeframe to do so. The State failed to comply in both cases with a clear attitude of complete disregard.

---

35. *See* Supreme Court, Arte Radiotelevisivo Argentino S. A. c/Estado Nacional—JGM—SMC s/amparo ley 16.986. Fallos, A. 925. XLIX., 11/02/14.
36. Supreme Court, Editorial Río Negro S.A c/Neuquén, Provincia del s/acción de amparo, Fallos, 330:3907.
37. Supreme Court, Editorial Perfil S.A. y otro c/E.N.—Jefatura Gabinete de Ministros—SMC s/amparo ley 16.986, Fallos, 334:109.

135. The Supreme Court noted the lack of compliance with prior decisions regarding the distribution of government advertising and concluded that it constituted a clear affront to the separation of powers, endangering the basis of Argentina's democracy. Although the case does not bring new elements in analyzing freedom of speech, it does strengthen the understandings developed in prior decisions and raises awareness around the lack of State compliance, which endangers not only freedom of speech protections in government advertising but the overall rule of law.

136. In conclusion, it could be noted that over the last decades, the Supreme Court has progressively included distinctions between private and public individuals, as well as between public and private interests, to provide greater protection for public interest and government-related debate. The Supreme Court has also developed doctrines that protect journalists and the general public from criminal and tort liability for defamation when it comes to information of public interest, as well as from the reproduction of information created by third parties. However, considering that most of these protections are jurisprudential and not legislative, the interpretation and relevance of such doctrines vary from case to case and lower courts do not fully adhere to the doctrines that have been developed.

137. Moreover, we can see that the Supreme Court has not always been consistent in its reasoning, and although some doctrines are well established, their content, scope and limitations are not.

Part II. Regulation of Print Media

138. There is no special regulation for the written press beyond the National Constitution. In fact, Article 32 limits the intervention of the State in this matter. As has been said, the basic regulation of the Argentine legal system in relation to the media is contained in the National Constitution. The National Constitution refers to the media by mentioning freedom of expression and the nonintervention of the State in the restriction of freedom of expression. This constitutional guarantee applies to all media: it covers from the written press to the Internet, but there is no specific regulation for the written press.

139. In 2009, the crimes of slander and libel were decriminalized, and previously (in 1993), the concept of contempt had been eliminated. As Argentina is a signatory of the Pact of San José de Costa Rica, which incorporates the right to reply, this figure may be requested. However, since it is not regulated at the national level, its application is minimal and extremely cumbersome.

140. There are also no national regulations on the regulation of official advertising (although there are provincial regulations in the provinces of Río Negro and Tierra del Fuego).

141. Finally, it can be said that in Argentina, there are no effective mechanisms for self-regulation of the press, nor codes of ethics that must be respected by those who practice journalism.

142. In general terms, it can be said that the written press has a minimum level of regulation only for the purpose of guaranteeing freedom of expression.

Chapter 1. The Journalists' Profession

143. In 1944, President Juan Domingo Perón enacted Decree 7618/44, which was confirmed in 1946 by Law 12,908, approving the "Statute for professional journalists" (as in Spanish "Estatuto para el Periodista Profesional").

144. For the purposes of such regulation, professional journalists are those persons who perform on a regular basis, for pecuniary remuneration, the tasks that are proper to them in daily or periodical publications and news agencies. Such are the director, co-director, deputy director, editor-in-chief, general secretary, editorial secretary, editorial assistant, news editor, editorialist, correspondent, editor, chronicler, reporter, cartoonist, translator, proofreader, graphic reporter, archivist, and permanent collaborator. This includes radio, film or television companies that broadcast, exhibit, or televise news or news of a journalistic nature, and only with respect to personnel engaged in these tasks.

145. A permanent collaborator is understood as one who works on a piecework basis in newspapers, periodicals, magazines, weeklies, yearbooks, and news agencies by means of articles or notes, with or without signature, remunerated pecuniarily per unit or per centimeters, when it reaches a minimum of twenty-four collaborations per year.

146. The advertising agents or brokers and accidental collaborators or outsiders to the profession are excluded from said law.

147. Those who take part in the editing of newspapers, periodicals, or magazines for ideological, political or trade union propaganda purposes, without receiving salaries, are neither considered professional journalists.

148. In order to practice journalism professionally, Law 12,908 establishes that registration in the national registry of journalists is mandatory with the following particularities: (i) registration must be granted within a term not exceeding fifteen days if the regulatory requirements have been met; (ii) during the entire registration process professional tasks may be performed, hiring being subject to the granting of registration; (iii) there is no obligation to register for those who intervene exclusively in publications that pursue only a commercial advertising purpose unrelated to the purposes of journalism in general.

149. Law 12,908 also provides that freedom of the press and thought are inalienable rights, and the professional license may not be denied, withdrawn, or canceled as a consequence of the opinions expressed by the journalist.

150. Specific studies or other qualities are not required in other to obtain the registration.

151. A special cause for denial of registration is to have suffered a judicial sentence that has not been declared suspended and while the effects of the sentence last.

152. Registration in the National Register of Journalists may only be canceled or suspended:

(a) If it has been obtained by trickery or deceit.
(b) By judicial sentence that has not been declared suspended and for the duration of the effects thereof.
(c) If the practice of the profession has been discontinued for two consecutive years.

153. The practice of nonprofessional journalism is not regulated in Argentina, and is protected by the right to freedom of expression provided for in the National Constitution and in the applicable international treaties.

154. However, Argentina does not have a legal position regarding bloggers. However, their posts are also included in the scope of the rules that protect freedom of speech.

155. In this sense, it should be noted that Decree 1279/97, referring to freedom of content, declares that the Internet service is included in the constitutional guarantee that protects freedom of speech, and Law 26,032 establishes that the search, reception and dissemination of information and ideas through the Internet service is included within the constitutional guarantee that protects freedom of speech.

Chapter 2. Journalists' Rights

§1. Role of Journalists as Watch-Dogs of Society

156. Journalism plays a relevant role in Argentine society, especially regarding investigative journalism on issues related to corruption, drug trafficking and other crimes.

157. Argentine society takes into special consideration the information it receives from the media, which gives journalistic work a preeminent influence in the nation.

158. Journalism played a leading role between 2007 and 2015 because of the confrontation between the Government of Cristina Fernández de Kirchner and Grupo Clarín, the main company that concentrates most of the printed and audiovisual media in the country.

159. During that stage, the existence of independent journalism began to be questioned, alleging from both sides that journalists did not have full editorial freedom with respect to the media group to which they belonged.

160. Debates on the independence of journalism continue to this day.

§2. Journalists' Independence

161. As said above, the independence of journalism is being challenged by both sides: political parties and private-owned companies.

162. Many people in Argentina believe that if a journalist is working in a state-owned media company, then he will be producing information only in favor of the government, and contrary, when the journalist belongs to certain media groups, such as Grupo Clarín, will be criticizing the government with no bases or fake news.

163. There are not specific regulations to protect journalists' independence in Argentina.

§3. Protection of Journalistic Sources

164. Journalistic sources have the highest protection in the Argentine legal system. In the last part of the third paragraph of Article 43 of the National Constitution (text incorporated in the reform of 1994), within the framework of the writ of protection of personal data based on the "Principle of Confidentiality," it is established as a vigorous and unprecedented protection of freedom of information, that "the secrecy of the sources of journalistic information may not be affected."

165. The most important antecedent of the constitutional rule is the rule determined by the Council of the European Community in 1973, with the consequent conceptual clarification of the adopted formula: *"professional secrecy consists of the journalist's right to refuse to reveal the identity of the author of the information to the employer, third parties and public or judicial authorities. But it is also the journalist's duty not to reveal publicly the sources of the information received in confidence."*

166. In the international system to which Argentina is a party, the ACHR explicitly establishes in Article 13 the guarantee of freedom of the press and freedom of expression in the broadest framework of the search for and dissemination of information, recognizing, in its first paragraph, that every person *"has the right to freedom of thought and expression. This right shall include freedom to seek, receive and impart information and ideas of all kinds, regardless of frontiers, either orally, in writing or in print, in the form of art, or through any other media of his choice."* The same article establishes the counterpart of this right, in the form of the obligation of the State and private parties not to *"restrict the right of expression by indirect means, such as the abuse of official or private controls of newsprint, radio frequencies, or equipment and apparatus used in the dissemination of information, or by any other means designed to impede the communication and circulation of ideas and opinions."* This is where, by way of inference, the protection of the secrecy of the identity of journalistic sources must be placed, since forcing the reporter to reveal their identity would constitute a case of indirect censorship.

167. However, the Declaration of Principles on Freedom of Expression, prepared by the Office of the Rapporteur for Freedom of Expression of the IACHR, stated in its eighth principle that: *"all social communicators have the right to reserve their sources of information, notes and personal and professional files."*

168. By acquiring constitutional hierarchy, the "professional secrecy of journalism" is placed in the highest part of our legal system, compulsory for the whole system of national and international legislation to which Argentina is a party. In that sense, Law 25,326 on "Protection of Personal Data" of the year 2000 established that "in no case may the database or the sources of journalistic information be affected" and it was specified that the protection extended to the journalist's data files as well as to those of the media.

169. In Argentine jurisprudence, it is worth noting that the notion that the professional secrecy of journalists is clearly different from that of other professions, such as medicine, for example, has been affirmed because the information from their sources is a sort of "basic input."

170. This basic element of journalistic production carries in its essence the trust that each informant places in each professional in particular, with whom he establishes a relationship different from that of other professionals with his client or patient; this is a relationship protected by its transcendent value for the "rule of law," which has as one of its essential characteristics the respect for freedom of expression, since the normal functioning of the press emerges as one of the guarantees of public control of government acts.

171. The Supreme Court of Justice of the Nation, in the case "Vago, Jorge v. Ediciones La Urraca" (1991),[38] emphasizes the importance of the protection of the "right to inform," recognizing the journalistic activity a decisive role in the normal functioning of the republican system of government:

> "The function of the press in a democratic republic pursues, among other main objectives, to inform the reader as objectively and truthfully as possible; to contribute to the elaboration of the popular will and to serve as a means of expression to the public opinion" that is why:
> "(...) the press cannot abandon its function as an essential factor for the clarification of the conduct of public officials, especially in countries such as ours, which lack an institutionalized body that assumes as a priority the defense of those interests qualified as diffuse. In such a way that, in practice, it acts as a means of control of the institutions and their men and renders a service of inestimable value for the strengthening and health of the republican system and institutions (...)" (Supreme Court of Justice of the Nation, 1991).

172. The statements of the Supreme Court state that the informative apparatus, in the construction of public opinion, must be totally independent from government action in order to guarantee its freedom of judgment.

173. As has already been expressed, we would find ourselves before the limits of the legitimate exercise of this right (to go beyond it would make it absolute to the detriment of other essential rights), since the professional secrecy of the journalist must yield to values such as the right to life, the right to freedom of an innocent person or the power to punish the perpetrator of a criminal act, higher interests of the community inherent to its existence as a legally organized community.

174. The ethical duty of the informant would change its polarity, given the seriousness of the facts and with a view to higher values, imposing on him the obligation to provide his source of information.

175. This is the solution—which arises by way of a *contrario sensu* interpretation—arrived at by the judges of the National Federal Criminal and Correctional Chamber, Chamber II, on 10/28/2002, in the case "Catan, Thomas s/ incidente."

38. *See* Supreme Court, "Vago, Jorge v. Ediciones La Urraca," 1991.

Chapter 3. Journalists' Liability

§1. General Information on the Liability System

176. Under the civil, commercial and consumer laws, the general rule of tortious liability is that all harm caused by negligent or wilfull, illicit acts must be indemnified. Strict and joint liability applies for cases of loss or injury caused by defective products or services.

177. Courts and authors have traditionally set out four requirements of tortious liability:

- Harm: the claimant must suffer actual property loss or injury.
- Illicit act: there must be an illicit act or a breach of a legal duty by the defendant.
- Causal relationship: a legally relevant cause and effect relationship must exist between the damage suffered by the claimant and the defendant's action.
- Attribution factor: the illegal act must be imputable to the wilfull or negligent conduct of the defendant.

178. Claimants can seek compensatory damages, loss of profit, moral damages, and punitive damages, among others.

179. The burden of proof lies, in principle, on the claimant. In cases of strict liability, the defendant must prove that it had no liability because the harm was in fact attributable to the claimant's conduct or a third party.

180. Causation is established by looking for the "adequate cause." Therefore, an act or omission resulting in damage will be attributed to a person if such act or omission can be proved to regularly or commonly lead to such result. Therefore, an abstract or objective foreseeability test is used to establish whether a given result is the consequence of a given act or omission. The cause must contribute effectively to the harm suffered.

§2. (Is There a Special Liability Regime for Journalists? Who Will Be Held Liable: Only the Journalist or Also the Publisher ... ?)

181. In Argentina, there is no specific liability system for journalists and the media. However, jurisprudence has recognized that there is joint and several liability between the journalist and the media to which he/she belongs. Thus, jurisprudence[39] usually extends sentences to pay damages to media companies for defamations incurred by their journalists. In those cases, it is usually considered that the media companies are negligent for not preventing the continuity of the news and/or not ensuring the right to immediate reply.

39. *See*, for example, National Chmabers of Appeals in Civil Matters, "N., M. F. c/Coop. de Trabajo Por Más Tiempo Ltda. y otros s/daños y perjuicios," judgment issued on Apr. 4, 2022.

§3. DEFAMATION AND LIBEL

182. Under Argentine law, slander and libel are typified in the Criminal Code as crimes against honor, which affect the prestige, dignity, and reputation of natural persons, under two different types of crimes: slander and libel.

183. To slander is to falsely accuse another of having committed a crime. It is not a crime if the statements relate to a matter of public interest. According to section 109 of the Criminal Code, the penalty is a fine of ARS 3,000 to ARS 30,000.

184. To injure is to intentionally dishonor or discredit a person. It is not a crime if the statements are related to a matter of public interest. According to section 110 of the Criminal Code, the penalty is a fine of ARS 1,500 to ARS 20,000.

185. When the media publish or reproduce slander or libel, no penalty is applied if they cite the source, i.e., if they publish who said it. They are also not subject to penalty if it is a matter of public interest. The offended party may ask the judge to order the publication of the sentence condemning the offender. If the person accused of libel or slander publicly retracts before the trial begins, he/she is exempt from punishment.

§4. PRIVACY

Privacy is One of the External Limits to Freedom of Speech

186. The right to privacy has been defined in doctrine as "the most personal right that protects the spiritual reserve of man's private life, ensuring the free development of his personal life"[40] and it is specified that it is "the innate, vital, necessary, extra-patrimonial and relatively available right that empowers its holder to: a) exclude third parties from intruding in the most arcane circle of the subject, b) avoid intrusions in that area and c) control the data and information related to his person and even to achieve the suppression, rectification, confidentiality or updating of those."

187. The sphere of private life includes not only the private actions of the individual himself but also those of his family. The protection of this private sphere is supported by Article 19 of the National Constitution, which states that *"the private actions of men that in no way offend public order and morals, nor harm a third party, are reserved only to God, and exempt from the authority of the magistrates."*

---

40. Zavala de González, M, *Resarcimiento de Daños: Daños a la Persona*, Integridad Espiritual y Social, Vol. 2d, 2da edición ampliada, 2da reimpresión, Buenos Aires (Argentina: Hammurabi 1996).

188. The private actions referred to in the aforementioned article are not only those that are carried out in private and without anyone knowing about them but also those that we could call "public" because they are externalized before third parties or are known by third parties, but without the capacity to harm the common good.

189. That is to say that both the activity that an individual develops in his home, as well as in the public thoroughfare, without affecting public order or morals or harming a third party, are protected from the intrusions of the State or private parties and therefore protected by the right to privacy.

190. The aforementioned intrusions are those that disturb intimacy and that cause individuals living in society to have "an attitude of prudent distance or discretion, so as not to otherwise harm customs or feelings concerning that intimate life."[41]

191. This implies that whoever does not maintain this type of conduct and takes an attitude of indiscretion towards the acts performed by an individual and his family is clearly violating the right to privacy of that person, and therefore, whoever is harmed by it is entitled to reverse things to their previous state, i.e., to assert his right to stop the vexatious conduct.

I. Regulatory Framework

192. In Argentina, there is no special law that specifically regulates the right to privacy. However, such regulatory framework can be drawn from:

(i) Articles 19 and 18 of the National Constitution, Article 11 of the Pact of San José de Costa Rica and Article 12 of the Declaration of Human Rights, both with constitutional hierarchy as of the 1994 reform.
(ii) Articles 52 and 1770 of the National Civil and Commercial Code.

II. Limitations

193. Although the right to privacy is a right inherent to a person by the mere fact of being a person, it may be reduced in the case of public persons or may be lacking in the case of dead persons and legal entities.

194. Cases of limitations to the right to privacy:

41. Zavala de González, 1982, p. 75.

1. Public Interest

195. The right to privacy is not absolute; this means that in situations where it is intended to ensure the public interest, the intrusion into the private life of a particular person becomes legitimate. The social interest mentioned must be "sufficiently serious and important to be considered superior."

196. In cases where the press transgresses the right to privacy of a person, in principle, such conduct is arbitrary, unless there is a public interest, which acts as a cause of justification enervating the unlawfulness of the action deployed by the media.

197. Likewise, an assessment must be made between the facts and the public interest, considering the circumstances of the particular case, and from there determine whether the right to privacy yields to the public interest or vice versa.

2. Consent

198. When the intrusion into the private life of a person has the consent of the same, it legitimizes the conduct and acts as an exemption from liability, if it does not amount to a contradiction with the law, morals and good customs or with the rights of a third party. Such consent must be unequivocal, tacit, or express and strictly interpreted.

199. The total and anticipated waiver of the right to privacy is not allowed, since it would affect public order, but the occasional waiver and for a price is allowed.

200. The holder of the affected right can freely revoke his consent at any time without any reason; in these cases, it should be analyzed if the injury generates any right of compensation of the expectations of the other party.

3. Situation of Necessity

201. The state of necessity as a limit to the right to privacy in cases where, in order to avoid a greater damage, the author reveals certain reserved aspects of the life of another person.

Chapter 4. Right to Reply

202. In Argentina, the right to reply is recognized in Article 14.1. of the ACHR (incorporated into our Constitution in Article 75, paragraph 22). This article reads as follows: *"Any person affected by inaccurate or offensive information issued to his detriment through the legally regulated media and which is addressed to the general public, has the right to have it corrected or replied to by the same media under the conditions established by law."*

203. The Inter-American Court of Human Rights, in its Advisory Opinion 7/86 of August 29, 1986, ruled on the enforceability of the right to reply in the following terms:

- Article 14.1 of the Inter-ACHR recognizes an internationally enforceable right of reply which, in accordance with Article 1.1, the State Parties have the obligation to respect and guarantee its free and full exercise to all persons subject to their jurisdiction.
- When the right of reply cannot be given effect in the domestic legal system of a state party, that State has the obligation to adopt, in accordance with its constitutional procedures and the provisions of the Convention itself, any other legislative measures that may be necessary.

204. The Inter-American Court of Human Rights did not rule on the possible content of domestic legislation.

205. The first case in which the Supreme Court of Justice of the Nation recognized the right to reply was "*Ekmedjian v. Sofovich,*" in 1992, in which that court ruled that a person who claimed to have been affected in his religious feelings by allegedly offensive statements against the Catholic Church, made during a television program, had the right to have his reply read in the same program. In that precedent, the Court understood that the right to reply was operative in the Argentine legal system and, therefore, directly enforceable and established a series of rules related to the nature of the right and the way in which it should be enforced:

- The right to reply has the purpose of clarification, free of charge and immediately in the face of information that causes damage to the dignity, honor, and intimacy of a person in the social communication media that disseminated them. As for its legal framework, it does not require the intent to slander or libel, nor the presupposition of criminal offense. It is not a matter of a lawsuit for slander or libel nor an action for damages.
- It is a subjective right of special character and exceptional recognition that requires, to enable its exercise, an offense of substantial gravity, that is, not a mere dissenting opinion with that held by the affected party, but a real offense generated in a superficial affirmation without even reasonable appearance of argumentative support.

- Its restorative effect reaches all those who may have felt equally offended by the same offense under the conditions that the legislator or the judge deems prudent to consider in order to prevent the recognized right from becoming a multiplication of endless responses.
- The reply or rectification does not admit its origin in cases of political or electoral opinions.
- The space that the response must occupy must not exceed the space appropriate to its purpose, and in no way must it necessarily be of the same extension and location as that of the initial publication, which must be interpreted in a context of reasonableness and good faith but avoiding an extensive interpretation of the institute that affects the protection of the exercise of the right to information.

206. Subsequently, in the "*Petric*" case, which was decided in 1998, the Court developed a much more restrictive criterion with respect to this right. On that occasion, the Court ruled, among other things, that the right to reply only existed with respect to "facts" and not "opinions." This meant a clear difference in relation to the "*Ekmekdjian*" case: while in that case, the Court had ruled that the alleged affectation of Ekmekdjian's "religious beliefs" gave rise to the right of reply in favor of the named person, in the "*Petric*" case it was said that only the assertion of "inaccurate or offensive" facts by the media (and that, in addition, it had to refer to an individual and specific person), could serve to recognize the right of reply.

Chapter 5. Access to Public Information

§1. Constitutional Framework

207. The right to access public information is implicitly recognized in section 1 of the National Constitution, which establishes that Argentina adopts a representative, republican and federal form of government. Doctrine and jurisprudence have held that the republican form of government implies the right of citizens to access public information.

208. Article 1 of the National Constitution must be complemented by Article 33, which establishes that the declarations, rights and guarantees enumerated in the Constitution shall not be understood as a denial of other rights and guarantees not enumerated but which arise from the principle of the sovereignty of the people and the republican form of government.

209. Beyond that, the right to access public information is recognized in international treaties with constitutional hierarchy according to the provisions of Article 75, paragraph 22 of the National Constitution.

210. In this sense, Article 13 of the ACHR defines the right to freedom of expression as the right to "seek, receive and impart information and ideas of all kinds," obviously including information held by the State. Thus, this Convention affirms the derivation of the right of access to information from the right to freedom of expression, understood not only as an individual right but also as a collective right.

211. Along the same interpretative line, Article 19 of the Universal Declaration of Human Rights protects the right of access to information by stipulating that "everyone has the right to freedom of opinion and expression" and that "this right includes freedom to hold opinions without interference and to seek, receive and impart information and ideas through any media and regardless of frontiers."

212. Article 19 of the International Covenant on Civil and Political Rights (ICCPR) also aims to protect access to information based on a reading of the right to freedom of expression as a collective right.

§2. Jurisprudential Developments

213. The right to access public information has been recognized by the jurisprudence of the Supreme Court of Justice of the Nation, which issued between 2012 and 2016 four transcendent rulings that validated the right of access to public information. In them, it recognized the principles governing this right and established the essential doctrine on the characteristics of the person obliged to provide the information, even if in strict terms it is not a state entity; the quality of the personal data that does not become "context-sensitive" and on the very broad legal standing recognized to "any member of the community."

214. In *Asociación por los Derechos Civiles v. PAMI*,[42] the plaintiff requested information from PAMI regarding the budget that the agency had allocated to official advertising and the distribution of such advertising. The defendant rejected the request on the grounds that Decree 1173/03, which regulated access to State documents, was not applicable to it, since the agency was not a State institution. Although this issue was beyond doubt, the Supreme Court dismissed the argument by stating that, despite not having "state nature," the PAMI, *"given its special characteristics and the important and transcendent public interests involved,"* must provide such information in the framework of a democratic society, since it is an institution that *"manages public interests and holds a delegated function of the State, being indisputable the interrelation between the defendant entity and the state administration."* As can be seen, the rule established by the Supreme Court considered that the case involved "information," since it met two concurrent requirements: (a) it involved data of public interest and (b) the entity—without being a State entity—exercised a function delegated by the State.

215. In the precedent "CIPPEC,"[43] the plaintiff requested, in 2008, from the Ministry of Social Security, data referring to: (a) the beneficiaries, intermediaries and distributors of social plans; (b) the application and execution of those social plans according to the budget; and (c) the territorial scope of the program. The State's refusal to inform was evasive and inconsistent. It claimed the right to privacy of the beneficiaries, guaranteed in the habeas data law; the protection of personal data, allegedly sensitive due to the context and, therefore, susceptible to generate stigmatization and discrimination. In this line, the Supreme Court rejected the argument by warning that the Administration did not act in good faith because: (a) the legal entities—social organizations that distribute the plans—do not have sensitive data referring to privacy; (b) it forgot the State's duty of "transparency and maximum disclosure"; the State's refusal assumed a certain form of "paternalism"; far from stigmatizing, the social control of effectiveness, efficiency and reasonableness contributes to assess the fairness of the social plans. As the Court pointed out, the limit for those who treat personal data does not apply when there is a legitimate interest, emphasizing that when the information serves to warn about the functionality or dysfunctionality of social policy and contributes to reveal, examine and evaluate the program, without closing the debate, to correct the shortcomings, if any. Weighing these interests, the interest of maximum disclosure prevails, and publicity must go through all stages of the State's actions in order to prevent impunity. Dr Petracchi's concurring vote illustrates with eminent erudition the transcendence and value of public information, indicating that *"… transparency, not opacity, benefits the vulnerable. Helping them is not ignominious, ignominy is pretending to hide*

42. *See*, Supreme Court, "Asociación por los Derechos Civiles v. EN—PAMI (decree 1173/03) s/amparo," C.S. A. 917. XLVI (2012) Consids. 7, 12 and 13 of the majority vote.
43. *See*, Supreme Court, "*CIPPEC v. National State—Ministry of Social Development*," (Judgments 337:256).

who is being assisted, pretending that secrecy prevails in the field of channelling public funds. Funds that, it seems unnecessary to clarify, do not belong to the Ministry but to society as a whole."

216. In the "*Giustiniani*" precedent,[44] the plaintiff requested a full copy of the investment project agreement that YPF SA had entered into with Chevron Corporation for the joint exploitation of hydrocarbons. The Supreme Court, in recognizing the petitioner's right, remarked that: (a) the National Executive Power has the authority to govern YPF, among other reasons because the general manager of the company was appointed by the President of the Nation; having been regulated in a decree that such entity was part of the National Public Sector, which did not prevent the company from being regulated by private law rules, *"in order to provide flexibility and speed in its management and operations"; (b) although this was not the case, Law 26,741—which declared of public utility and subject to expropriation 51% of YPF's assets—also considered of "national public interest" the achievement of self-supply of hydrocarbons as a priority objective of the Argentine Republic, and, (c) as a consequence, "the company performs important and transcendental activities, in which the public interest is compromised, so it cannot, within the framework of the principles of a democratic society and according to the reserved jurisprudence, deny information of undoubted public interest, which makes the transparency and publicity of its management."* In this precedent, the Supreme Court expressly admitted that the right of access to public information of public interest or under State control is not absolute. However, it maintained a reasonable rule in this regard, in order *"not to render illusory the principle of maximum disclosure prevailing in the matter,"* by considering that the parties obliged to provide the information may only refuse the request *"if they expose, describe and demonstrate in detail the elements and reasons why its delivery is likely to cause damage to the legitimately protected purpose."*

217. Finally, in the precedent "Garrido,"[45] in his capacity as congressman and citizen, he filed his action in order to obtain information on the appointment of an Federal Tax Agency agent and the status of the administrative investigation that had been carried out against such agent for alleged smuggling. The Supreme Court, in the same direction as in "CIPPEC," held that in the matter of the right of access to public information, the standing is broad; it is sufficient to be a "member of the community." In other words, every person, every inhabitant, has this right. This is the consecration of the popular action in the matter.

---

44. *See*, Supreme Court, "*Giustiniani, Rubén Héctor v. Y.P.F. S.A.* s/amparo for delay," (Judgments 338:1258).
45. *See*, Supreme Court, "*Garrido, Carlos Manuel v. EN—AFIP s/amparo Ley 16.986*," (Judgments: 339:827).

§3. ACCESS TO PUBLIC INFORMATION LAW

218. Because of the jurisprudential evolution, in 2016, Law No. 27,275 was enacted in Argentina, which recognizes and regulates the right of access to public information, which came into force one year after its publication in the Official Gazette of the Argentine Republic. Although there were already regulations that contemplated this right since 2003 (through Decree No. 1172/03), it was only in force within the scope of the National Executive Branch.

219. Law No. 27,275 extended its scope of application to other branches and agencies of the State, since it applies to the national public administration; the Legislative Branch; the National Judicial Branch; the National Public Prosecutor's Office; the Public Defender's Office; the Council of the Judiciary; State companies and corporations; concessionaires, permit holders and licensees of public services and public domain use; business organizations, political parties, unions, universities and any private entity to which public funds have been granted; concessionaires, permit holders and licensees of public services and use of the public domain; business organizations, political parties, trade unions, universities and any private entity to which public funds have been granted; institutions or funds whose administration, custody or conservation is in charge of the national State; non-State public legal entities with respect to information produced or related to public funds received; trusts totally or partially constituted with resources or assets of the National State, cooperating entities with which the national public administration has entered into or enters into agreements for the purpose of technical or financial cooperation with State agencies; the Central Bank of the Argentine Republic; inter-jurisdictional entities in which the National State has participation or representation; and concessionaires, exploiters, managers and operators of games of chance, skill and betting duly authorized by the competent authority.

220. The purpose of the law is to guarantee the effective exercise of the right of access to public information and to promote citizen participation and transparency in public management.

221. To make the law operational, a decalogue of principles is established to interpret the right of access to public information, from which the real and unconditional empowerment of the citizenry can be glimpsed:

- Presumption of publicity: all information held by the State is presumed to be public, subject to the exceptions provided for.
- Transparency and maximum disclosure: all information in the possession, custody or control of the regulated entity must be accessible to all persons.
- Informalism: the procedural rules for accessing information must facilitate the exercise of the right and their nonobservance may not constitute an obstacle to this.
- Maximum access: the information must be published in a complete manner, with the highest possible level of disaggregation and by the greatest possible number of available means.

- Openness: the information must be accessible in open electronic formats, which facilitate its processing by automatic means that allow its reuse or redistribution by third parties.
- Dissociation: in those cases in which part of the information falls within the exceptions established by this law, the non-excepted information must be published in a version of the document that crosses out, hides or dissociates those parts subject to the exception.
- Nondiscrimination: information must be provided to all persons who request it, without requiring an expression of cause or reason for the request.
- Maximum haste: information must be published as quickly as possible and in a time frame compatible with the preservation of its value.
- Free of charge: access to information must be free of charge, without prejudice to the provisions of this law.
- Control: Resolutions denying requests for access to information, such as the silence of the requested obligated subject, ambiguity, or inaccuracy of its response, may be appealed before the competent body.
- Liability: Failure to comply with the obligations imposed by this law will give rise to liability and the corresponding sanctions.
- Limited scope of exceptions: limits to the right of access to public information must be exceptional, previously established in accordance with the provisions of this law, and formulated in clear and precise terms, leaving the responsibility of demonstrating the validity of any restriction to access to information to the subject from whom the information is required.
- *In dubio pro petitor*: the interpretation of the provisions of this law or of any regulation of the right of access to information must be made, in case of doubt, always in favor of the greater validity and scope of the right to information.
- Facilitation: no public authority may refuse to indicate whether a document is in its possession or refuse to disclose a document in accordance with the exceptions contained in this law, unless the harm caused to the protected interest outweighs the public interest in obtaining the information.
- Good faith: to guarantee the effective exercise of access to information, it is essential that the regulated entities act in good faith, that is, that they interpret the law in such a way that it serves to fulfill the purposes pursued.

222. Likewise, the law (Article 2) establishes that all information generated, obtained, transformed, controlled, or kept by the regulated entities covered by this law is presumed to be public.

223. Regarding the delicate issue of standing to request access to public information, the norm in comment stipulates in Article 4 that any human or legal person, public or private, has the right to request and receive public information, and the applicant cannot be required to justify the request, to prove a subjective right or legitimate interest or to have legal counsel. This is in line with the decision of the CSJN, in the precedent "Garrido," when defining that in matters of right of access to public information, the legal standing is broad; it is enough to be "a member of the community."

224. To promote maximum disclosure, the information must be provided in the state in which it is at the time the request is made, and the requested party is not obliged to process or classify it. The State is obliged to deliver it in open digital formats, except in exceptional cases.

225. Section 7 of the law determines its scope of application, taking a broad criterion, by establishing as obligated subjects the so-called branches of government and extra-public bodies obliged to provide information: the National Public Administration, comprising the central administration, decentralized agencies and social security institutions; the Legislative Branch and the bodies that operate within its scope; the National Judicial Branch; the Public Prosecutor's Office; and the Public Defender's Office and the Magistrates Council. The following are also obliged subjects: State companies and corporations, corporations with a majority State shareholding and all those business organizations with equal State shareholding in the capital or in the formation of corporate decisions. However, if the State has a minority participation, it is bound by the law, but only with respect to that participation. Likewise, concessionaires, permit holders and licensees of public services or concessionaires of public domain use are bound by the law to the extent that they perform public services and in all that corresponds to the exercise of the delegated administrative function, and contractors, suppliers and service providers under any other contractual form or modality are bound by the law as well as concessionaires, exploiters, administrators and operators of games of chance, skill and betting, duly authorized by the competent authority.

226. All business organizations, political parties, trade unions, universities, or private entities to which public funds have been provided are obliged subjects, as far as those funds are concerned. The Professional Associations with registration control are included among the *"non-state public legal entities, obliged in all matters regulated by public law,"* as well as in the case in which they receive public funds.

227. Also, institutions or funds whose administration, custody, or conservation is in charge of the National State are cooperating entities with which the National Public Administration has entered into agreements whose purpose is technical or financial cooperation with state agencies. The Central Bank of the Argentine Republic and the interjurisdictional entities in which the National State has participation or representation.

228. As can be seen, the list is broad, but according to the postulates of the law, it is not exhaustive. State participation in other cases not provided for in the law, in accordance with the principle of presumption of publicity, will require the provision of information, but not limited to the extent of its participation.

229. The law establishes the exceptions on which the parties obliged to provide the information may rely upon in order not to comply with the requirement. In accordance with the protective purpose set forth in the law and the principles established in this regard, such exceptions must be weighed with a highly restrictive criterion resulting from a reasonable and reasoned judgment of the authority that invokes it.

230. The grounds listed as limitations to the obligation to inform arise from section 8 of the law and may come from other regulatory provisions; the reservation of information classified as confidential or secret for reasons of defense or foreign policy; information that could endanger the financial or banking system, industrial, commercial, financial, scientific, or technical secrets that could endanger the competitiveness or the interests of the obliged subject. Professional secrecy and information referring to personal data that cannot be dissociated are also protected. Information that may endanger the life or safety of persons, information of a judicial nature forbidden by other laws or commitments undertaken by the Argentine Republic in international treaties, information obtained in investigations carried out by the regulated entities that are confidential and whose dissemination could frustrate them.

I. Public Documents and Meetings

231. Public documents and meetings are under the scope of Law No. 27,275. *We refer to prior chapter.*

II. Court Hearings and Documents

232. Court hearings and documents are under the scope of Law No. 27,275. *We refer to prior chapter.*

Chapter 6. Press Council

233. The Association of Argentine Journalism Entities (*Asociación de Entidades Periodísticas Argentinas* (ADEPA), by its acronym in Spanish) is a national non-profit organization founded in 1962; currently, it brings together 180 media companies across the country, newspaper publishers, newspapers, magazines, and websites. ADEPA is now the most representative institution of national journalism.

234. Since its inception, the organization has played an increasingly active role in the defense and promotion of press freedom, the cornerstone of the Argentine democratic and republican systems. Thanks to this, ADEPA has become an umbrella of protection against attacks on the press and anyone who wants to express themselves freely. It also urges legal action in defense of press freedom, the right to information and the independence of the newspaper industry.[46]

235. In addition, as part of its collective and institutional actions, ADEPA has established itself as a space in which media representatives across the country can exchange experiences and knowledge about the industry; reporters, photographers and illustrators are encouraged and recognized through its annual awards; they are trained, and alerted about new trends in the newspaper industry, technological convergence, and ways to adapt to them.

46. Actions taken by ADEPA are available at its official web page: https://adepa.org.ar/.

Part III. Regulation of Audiovisual Media (Broadcasting)

Chapter 1. Public Service Broadcasting

§1. The Concept and Mission of Public Service Broadcasting

236. Public service broadcasting (PSB) is regulated by Law 26,522 enacted on October 10, 2010, and published in the Official Gazette on the same date, and deeply amended by the Necessity and Urgency Decree (*Decreto de Necesidad y Urgencia* furnished with the same hierarchy of a law enacted from the National Congress) 267/15 (Official Gazette December 23, 2015) referred to above (Media Law).

237. The purpose of this law is the regulation of PSB—or audiovisual communication services, as named by said law—throughout the territory of the Argentine Republic and the development of mechanisms for the promotion, deconcentrating and promotion of competition for the purposes of cheaper, democratized, and universalized use of the new information and communication technologies (section 1).

238. All emissions originating in the national territory, as well as those generated abroad when they are retransmitted or distributed there, are included in the provisions of this law (section 1).

239. The activity carried out by PSB providers is an activity of public interest, fundamental to the socio-cultural development of the population, through which the inalienable human right to express, receive, disseminate, and investigate information, ideas and opinions is expressed. PSB may be carried out by state-managed, privately managed for profit and privately managed nonprofit providers, who must have the capacity to operate and have equitable access to all transmission platforms available (section 2).

240. The condition of activity of public interest is based on the obligations of the National Congress established in Article 75, paragraph 19 of the National Constitution, which entitles the National State to override the Provinces' right to regulate the matter to safeguard the right to information, participation, preservation, and development of the rule of law, as well as the values of freedom of expression (section 2).

241. Among the objectives of the Media Law (section 3), the following could be highlighted:

(a) The promotion and guarantee of the free exercise of the right to investigate, seek, receive and disseminate information, opinions and ideas, without censorship, within the framework of respect for the democratic rule of law and human rights, in accordance with emerging obligations of the ACHR (*Convención Americana sobre Derechos Humanos*) and other treaties incorporated or that would be incorporated in the future to the National Constitution.
(b) The promotion of federalism and Latin American Regional Integration.
(c) The dissemination of the guarantees and fundamental rights enshrined in the National Constitution.
(d) The defense of the human being and respect of his and/ or her personal rights.
(e) The construction of an information and knowledge society that prioritizes media literacy and the elimination of gaps in access to knowledge and new technologies.
(f) The promotion of the expression of popular culture and the cultural, educational and social development of the population.
(g) The exercise of the inhabitants' right to access public information.
(h) The performance of media activities based on ethical principles.
(i) The participation of media as trainers of human beings, social actors and different ways of understanding life and the world, with a plurality of points of view and full debate of ideas.
(j) The strengthening of actions that contribute to the cultural, artistic and educational development of the cities where those actions are deployed and the production of formal strategies of mass and distance education, the latter under the control of the corresponding educational jurisdictions.
(k) The balanced development of a national content industry that preserves and disseminates the cultural heritage and diversity of all the regions and cultures which integrate the Nation.
(l) The administration of the radioelectric spectrum based on democratic and republican criteria that guarantee equal opportunities of access for all individuals.
(m) Promote the protection and safeguarding of equality between men and women, and plural, egalitarian and non-stereotyped treatment, avoiding all discrimination based on gender or sexual orientation.
(n) The right of access to information and content for people with disabilities.
(o) The preservation and promotion of the identity and cultural values of the Native Peoples.

242. Decree 1225/2010 (Official Gazette September 1, 2010—"Decree 1225/10") further regulates paragraph h) above, establishing the objective foreseen therein involves the self-regulation and the observance of ethical principles in informative matters and the adoption of good practices in the exercise of the communicational activity by the PSB licensees.

§2. THE ORGANIZATION OF PSB

243. Decree 267/15 amended PSB and telecommunication authorities, merging them into a unique and integrated authority covering both converging markets, repealing what were two complex and numerous regulatory bodies with the intervention of several stakeholders which finally resulted in a political control by the Executive Branch.

244. As established by Media Law and ICT Law, as amended by Decree 267/15, the ENACOM is currently the competent authority overseeing PSB and telecommunication markets.

245. ENACOM is not an independent body since the majority of its members are appointed and can be removed by the Executive Branch.

246. Regarding PSB, ENACOM's missions and functions are (section 12 Media Law):

(i) Apply, interpret and enforce Media Law and its regulatory rules.
(ii) Integrate national State delegations acting before international organizations and participate in the elaboration and negotiation of treaties, agreements or international broadcasting and telecommunications conventions as far as relevant to the Media Law.
(iii) Prepare and update the National Service Standard and the technical standards that regulate the activity.
(iv) Promote the participation of PSB in the development of the Information and Knowledge Society.
(v) Approve the technical projects of the broadcasting stations, grant the corresponding authorization, and approve the start of regular transmissions in conjunction with the regulatory authority and the enforcement authority in telecommunications matters.
(vi) Prepare and approve the terms and conditions for the awarding of PSB licenses.
(vii) To substantiate the procedures for tenders, direct award and authorization, as appropriate, for the exploitation of PSB.
(viii) Award and extend, where appropriate, and declare the expiration of licenses, permits and authorizations, subject to full and timely judicial control, including precautionary measures.
(ix) Supervise and verify compliance with the obligations set forth in Media Law and the commitments assumed by PSB providers.
(x) Promote and stimulate competition and investment in the sector. Prevent and discourage monopolistic practices, anticompetitive, predatory and/ or abuse of a dominant position within the framework of the functions assigned to this body or others with competence in the matter.
(xi) Apply the corresponding sanctions for noncompliance with Media Law, its regulations, and its administrative acts under full and timely judicial control, including precautionary measures.

(xii) Declare the illegality of the stations and/ or broadcasts and promote the consequent judicial action, including precautionary measures, adopting the necessary measures to achieve the cessation of emissions declared illegal.
(xiii) Supervise, receive and administer the funds from taxes, fees and fines, and administer the assets and resources of the ENACOM.
(xiv) Resolve the appeals and claims of the public or other interested parties in administrative instances.
(xv) Modify, on legal or technical grounds, the technical parameters granted to a license, permit or authorization for the registered services.
(xvi) Periodically carry out technical studies to evaluate the level and effects of radioelectric emissions in the human body and in the environment in order to prevent all types of emissions that are harmful to health or cause environmental damage in order to put in the knowledge of the competent authorities.

247. The ENACOM will be subject to control of the General Audit Office of the Nation. It is a permanent and inexcusable obligation of the board of directors to give its acts publicity and transparency in matters of resources, expenses, personnel appointments and hiring.

I. Federal Council for Audiovisual Communication

248. The Media Law also created the Federal Council for Audiovisual Communication (*Consejo Federal de Comunicación Audiovisual*), a non-binding consulting entity receiving advice in connection with the PSB and the interest of boys, girls, and adolescents (section 17) and the Bicameral Commission for the Promotion and Monitoring of Audiovisual Communication (*Comisión Bicameral de Promoción y Seguimiento de la Comunidad Audiovisual*), integrated by eight national senators and eight national congressmen (section 18).

II. Bicameral Commission

249. The commission is in charge of proposing:

- Three members of ENACOM's board of directors, three members of the Argentina Radio and Televisión State-owned corporation (*Radio y Televisión Argentina Sociedad del Estado (RTA S.E.)*) board of directors, representing the following: one on behalf of the majority or the first minority in absence of it, one on behalf of the first or second minority, as the case may be, and one on behalf of the next minority.
- The PSB Public Defender.

250. It is also in charge of receiving and evaluating the report presented by the Honorary Advisory Council of Public Media (*Consejo Consultivo Honorario de los*

Medios Públicos), ensuring compliance with the provisions relating to Argentine Radio and Television, and evaluating the performance of the PSB Public Defender, as well as its removal petition.

III. PSB Public Defender

251. PSB Public Defender is created by the Media Law (section 19), setting forth the following missions and functions:

(a) Receive and channel inquiries, claims and complaints from the PSB public, having judicial and extrajudicial legitimacy to act ex officio, by itself and/ or on behalf of third parties, before all kinds of administrative or judicial authority.
(b) Keep a record of the queries, claims and complaints submitted by users publicly or privately.
(c) Convene public or private intermediate organizations, study and research centers or other entities of public good in general to create a participatory environment for permanent debate on the development and operation of the media.
(d) To monitor the claims and complaints presented and inform the competent authorities, interested parties, the press and the general public about their results and publish them.
(e) Submit to the Bicameral Commission an annual report of its actions.
(f) Convene public hearings in different regions of the country in order to evaluate the proper functioning of the broadcasting media and participate in those provided by the present or called by the authorities in the matter.
(g) Propose modifications of regulatory norms in the areas related to its competence or judicially question the legality or reasonableness of existing ones or those that will be issued in the future.
(h) To formulate public recommendations to the authorities with competence in the matter of broadcasting which will be of obligatory treatment.
(i) Represent the interests of the public and the community, individually or as a whole, in administrative or judicial headquarters, with procedural legitimacy by virtue of which it can request the annulment of general or particular acts, the issuance, modification or substitution of acts, and other precautionary or substantive requests necessary for the best performance of its function.

252. The Public Defender will express itself through public recommendations to the owners, authorities or professionals of the social communication media contemplated in this law or administrative or judicial presentations in which they are ordered to adjust their behavior to the legal system as soon as they depart from it, in the cases that occur.

253. The delegations of the enforcement authority must receive and channel claims addressed to the Public Defender.

254. The head of the Public Defender's Office will be appointed by a joint resolution of both Houses (Senate and Representatives) at the proposal of the Commission for the Promotion and Monitoring of PSB. His mandate will be four years and may be renewed only once. He or she may be removed for noncompliance or poor performance of his position by the National Congress after the opinion of the Commission for the Promotion and Monitoring of PSB, in a procedure in which the right of defense shall be guaranteed. The resolution adopted in this regard must be duly founded (section 20).

IV. National State Controlled PSB

255. The Media Law creates, under the jurisdiction of the national Executive Power, RTA S.E., which oversees the administration, operation, development and exploitation of sound and television broadcasting services of the national State (section 119).

256. The performance of RTA S.E. is subject to the provisions of Law 20,705 (rules the national State-owned corporations), the Media Law and its complementary provisions. In its external legal relations, property acquisitions and contracting are subject to the general regimes of private law (section 120).

257. The objectives of Radio and Television Argentina Sociedad del Estado are (section 121):

(1) Promote and develop respect for the human rights enshrined in the National Constitution and in the Declarations and Conventions incorporated therein.
(2) Respect and promote political, religious, social, cultural, linguistic and ethnic pluralism.
(3) Guarantee the right to information of all the inhabitants of the Argentine Nation.
(4) Contribute to the formal and non-formal education of the population, with programs aimed at its different social sectors.
(5) Promote the development and protection of the national identity within the multicultural framework of all the regions that make up the Argentine Republic.
(6) Allocate spaces to programming content dedicated to children, as well as to sectors of the population not covered by the commercial sector.
(7) Promote the production of its own audiovisual content and contribute to the dissemination of regional, national, and Latin American audiovisual production.
(8) Promote the cultural formation of the inhabitants of the Argentine Republic within the framework of Latin American regional integration.
(9) Guarantee the coverage of audiovisual communication services (ACS) throughout the national territory.

258. For the realization of the stated objectives, RTA S.E. will comply with the following obligations (section 122):

(1) Include in its programming, educational, cultural, and scientific contents that promote and strengthen the training and education of all social sectors.
(2) Produce and distribute content through different technological supports to meet its communication objectives, targeting audiences located within and outside the national territory.
(3) Permanently consider the social role of the communication medium as the foundation of its creation and existence.
(4) Ensure information and communication with adequate coverage of issues of national, regional, and international interest.
(5) Disseminate and promote artistic, cultural, and educational productions that are generated in the regions of the country.
(6) Disseminate the activities of the powers of the State at the national, provincial, Autonomous City of Buenos Aires and municipal levels.
(7) Install repeaters throughout the national territory and create national or regional networks.
(8) Celebrate cooperation, exchange, and reciprocal support agreements with public or private, national, and international entities, especially with the member countries of Mercosur.
(9) Offer access, in a global way, through the participation of significant social groups as sources and bearers of information and opinion in all the programming of Radio and Television Argentina Sociedad del Estado.

259. Radio and Television Argentina Sociedad del Estado must broadcast at least sixty percent (60%) of its own production and twenty percent (20%) of independent productions in all the media under its responsibility (section 123).

260. The direction and administration of RTA S.E. will be in charge of a Board of Directors made up of seven members. They must be people of the highest professional qualification in communication matters and have a democratic and recognized track record. The composition of the Board of Directors must guarantee due pluralism in the operation of the station (sections 131 and 132).

261. The Board of Directors will be made up of: One President appointed by the national Executive Power, One Director appointed by the national Executive Power, Three directors at the proposal of the Bicameral Commission for the Promotion and Monitoring of Audiovisual Communication, and who will be selected by it at the proposal of the parliamentary blocks of the political parties, one corresponding to the first minority, one to the second minority and one to the third parliamentary minority. Two of them are proposed by the Federal Council of Audiovisual Communication, one of them must be an academic representative of the faculties or careers of information sciences, communication sciences or journalism of national universities. The president of the board of directors is the legal representative of RTA S.E., who is in charge of presiding and calling the meetings of the Board of

Directors, according to the regulations. They will last four years in their positions and may be reelected for a period (sections 131 and 132).

262. The formation of the Board of Directors will be carried out within the two years prior to the end of the mandate of the Head of the national Executive Power, and there must be two years of difference between the beginning of the mandate of the Directors and the national Executive Power. The removal will be carried out in accordance with the statutory clauses (sections 131 and 132).

263. Without prejudice to the application of the incompatibilities or disqualifications established for the exercise of public function, the exercise of the positions of president and directors of Radio and Television Argentina Sociedad del Estado will be incompatible with the performance of political party directive and/ or elective positions, or any form of corporate relationship with journalistic companies and/ or electronic media of social communication created or to be created and/ or the provision of services linked to those that will be provided in RTA S.E. (section 133).

264. The activities of Radio and Television Argentina Sociedad del Estado will be financed with: (a) Twenty percent of the tax created by the Media Law, under the distribution conditions established by it; (b) Budgetary allocations attributed in the National Budget Law; (c) Sale of advertising; (d) The commercialization of its audiovisual content production; (e) Sponsorships or sponsorships; (f) Legacies, donations and any other source of financing resulting from events held in accordance with the objectives of RTA S.E. and its legal capacity. The Banco de la Nación Argentina will automatically and daily transfer to RTA S.E. the amount of the tax collected. The funds collected will be intangible, except in relation to labor credits recognized by final judgment with res judicata authority (section 136). Radio and Television Argentina Sociedad del Estado stations will be exempt from paying the taxes and/ or fees established in the Media Law (section 137).

265. The operation of Radio and Television Argentina Sociedad del Estado will be controlled by the General Audit Office of the Nation and the General Auditor of the Nation. It is a permanent and inexcusable obligation of the board of directors to give its acts the greatest publicity and transparency in matters of resources, expenses, staff appointments and hiring (section 139).

V. Honorary Advisory Council of Public Media

266. The Honorary Advisory Council of the Public Media will exercise social control of compliance with the objectives of this law by Radio and Televisión Argentina Sociedad del Estado and will function as an extra-scale consultative. It will be made up of members of recognized trajectory in the fields of culture, education or communication of the country (section 124).

267. They will be designated by the national Executive Power according to the following procedure: (a) two at the proposal of the Faculties and careers of Social or Audiovisual Communication or Journalism of national universities; (b) three at the proposal of the unions with union status in the sector with the largest number of members working in RTA S.E. at the time of appointment; (c) two by non-governmental human rights organizations or representatives of public or audiences; (d) six at the proposal of the jurisdictional governments of the geographic regions of the NOA; NEA; Whose; Center; Patagonia; Province of Buenos Aires and the Autonomous City of Buenos Aires; (e) one at the proposal of the Federal Council of Education; (f) two at the proposal of the Advisory Council for Audiovisual Communication and Children representing entities or organizations of producers of educational, children's or documentary television content; (g) one at the proposal of the Native Peoples (section 124).

268. The performance of positions in the Honorary Advisory Council of Public Media will last two years, and its members may be reelected by their respective entities. Such performance will be honorary, and no remuneration will be received for the task performed (section 125).

269. The Honorary Advisory Council of the Public Media shall meet at least every two months or extraordinarily at the request of at least 25% of its members. The quorum will be made up, both in ordinary and extraordinary calls, with an absolute majority of the total of its members. The meetings of the Honorary Advisory Council of the Public Media will be public. The preparation of a report regarding the issues considered and its publicity through the stations that make up RTA S.E. will be mandatory. In order to guarantee the better functioning of the Honorary Advisory Council of Public Media, the board of directors of RTA S.E. will assign the physical, financial and human resources it deems necessary for its management (sections 127, 128 and 129).

270. The Council is responsible for: (a) calling public hearings to evaluate the programming, content and operation of RTA S.E.; (b) contributing proposals destined to improve the operation of Radio and Television Argentina Sociedad del Estado; (c) enabling direct communication channels with citizens regardless of their geographic location and socioeconomic level; (d) supervising compliance with the objectives of creation of the Media law and report its breach before the Bicameral Commission for the Promotion and Monitoring of Audiovisual Communication; (e) convening the members of the board of directors of RTA S.E. every six months in order to receive a management report; (f) presenting their conclusions regarding the management report presented by the board of directors, to the Bicameral Commission for the Promotion and Monitoring of Audiovisual Communication (section 130).

VI. University and Educational Media

271. National universities and university institutes may be holders of authorizations for the installation and operation of broadcasting services. The enforcement authority will directly grant the corresponding authorization (section 145).

272. Those services will be financed with resources from: (a) budgetary allocations attributed to the national budget laws and in the university's own budget; (b) sale of advertising; (c) resources from the National Interuniversity Council or the Ministry of Education; (d) donations and legacies and any other source of financing resulting from events held in accordance with the objectives of the university broadcasting station and its legal capacity; (e) the sale of self-produced content; (f) sponsorships (section 146).

273. Broadcasters belonging to national universities may establish permanent programming networks among themselves or with state-run broadcasters in order to adequately meet their objectives (section 147).

274. University broadcasters must dedicate relevant spaces in their programming to the dissemination of scientific knowledge, university extension and artistic and cultural creation and experimentation. University radio stations must include in their programming a minimum of 60% of their own production (section 148).

275. The enforcement authority may grant, directly for well-founded reasons, authorizations for the operation of broadcasting services to state-run educational establishments. The holder of the authorization will be the jurisdictional educational authority, which will select for each locality the establishments that may operate the audiovisual communication service (section 149). The programming of ACS authorized accordingly must respond to the educational and institutional project of the educational establishment and must contain at least 60% of its own production. They will be able to freely retransmit the broadcasts of the member stations of Radio and Television Argentina Sociedad del Estado (section 150).

VII. Native Peoples Media

276. The Native Peoples may be authorized to install and operate PSB by sound broadcasting with AM and FM as well as open television broadcasting under the terms and conditions established in this law. The rights provided for in this law will be exercised in the terms and scope of Law 24,071, which approved the Convention 169 Of The International Labor Organization On Indigenous And Tribal Peoples In Independent Countries, adopted in Geneva, Switzerland, at the 76th Meeting of the International Labor Conference, whose certified copy is part of this law (section 151).

277. The services contemplated in this title will be financed with resources from: (a) allocations from the national budget; (b) sale of advertising; (c) donations, legacies and any other source of financing resulting from events held in accordance with the objectives of the communication service and its legal capacity; (d) the sale of self-produced content; (e) sponsorships or sponsorships; (f) specific resources assigned by the National Institute of Indigenous Affairs (section 152).

§3. The Financing of PSB

278. The holders of PSB services will pay a tax proportional to the amount of the gross billing corresponding to the commercialization of traditional and nontraditional advertising, programs, signals, content, subscriptions, and any other concept derived from the exploitation of these services. The income from contests, raffles and other activities or practices of a similar nature, except for those organized by official entities, will be taxed with the aliquots consigned in the "Other Services" category (section 94).

279. The signal registry holders will pay a tax proportional to the amount of the gross billing corresponding to the commercialization of spaces and advertisements of any kind in content broadcast in any of the services regulated by the Media Law. From the gross invoicing, only the commercial discounts and discounts in force in the market and that are actually invoiced and accounted for will be deductible (section 94).

280. The statute of limitation of the actions to determine and demand the payment of the tax, the interests and the updates established by the Media Law, as well as the action of repetition of them, operate after five years, counted as of January 1 following the year in which the obligations or the lien is due (section 95).

281. The calculation for the payment of the tax will be made according to the following categories and percentages (section 96):

I. Category A: services with a delivery area in the Autonomous City of Buenos Aires.
Category B: services with a delivery area in cities with six hundred thousand (600,000) or more inhabitants.
Category C: services with a delivery area in cities with less than six hundred thousand (600,000) inhabitants.
Category D: services with a delivery area in cities with less than one hundred thousand (100,000) inhabitants.

II. a) Open television.
Medium and high-power Category A 5%
Medium and high-power Category B 3.5%
Medium and high-power Category C 2.5%
Medium and high-power Category D 2%

b) Sound broadcasting.

AM Category A 2.5%
AM Category B 1.5%
AM Category C 1%
AM Category D 0.5%
FM Category A 2.5%
FM Category B 2%
FM Category C 1.5%
FM Category D 1%

c) Broadcast television and low power AM/ FM radio.
Category A and B 2%
Category C and D 1%
d) Satellite services by subscription 5%.
e) Non-satellite subscription services.
Category A 5%
Category B 3.5%
Category C 2.5%
Category D 2%
f) Signals
Foreign 5%
Nationals 3%
g) Other products and services
Category A and B 3%
Category C and D 1.5%

282. The funds collected will be applied as follows (section 97):

(a) Twenty-five percent of the total collected will be assigned to the National Institute of Cinema and Audiovisual Arts (Instituto Nacional de Cine y Artes Audiovisuales).
(b) Ten percent to the National Theater Institute. As a minimum, an equal amount received by virtue of Decree 2278/2002 as of the date of promulgation of this law must be assigned to the National Theater Institute (Instituto Nacional del Teatro).
(c) Twenty percent to RTA S.E. created by this law.
(d) Twenty-eight percent to the ENACOM, including funds for the operation of the Federal Council for Audiovisual Communication (Consejo Federal de Comunicación Audiovisual).
(e) Five percent for the operation of the Public Defender of Audiovisual Communication Services (Defensoría del Público de Servicios de Comunicación Audiovisual).
(f) Ten percent for special audiovisual communication projects and support for ACS, community, border, and Native Peoples, with special attention to collaboration in digitization projects.
(g) Two percent to the National Institute of Music (Instituto Nacional de Música).

283. In order to promote a federal distribution of the PSB, the enforcement authority may provide temporary exemptions or reductions of the abovementioned tax in the following circumstances (section 98):

(a) The holders of licenses or authorizations for television services located outside the Buenos Aires metropolitan area that directly produce or locally acquire works of fiction or audiovisual arts, of any genre, format or duration, may deduct from the tax instituted by this law up to 30% of the amount to be paid for this concept during the fiscal period corresponding to the broadcast time at the premiere of the work in the service operated by the owner.
(b) Holders of PSB located in border areas and zones will enjoy an exemption from paying the tax during the first five years from the start of their broadcasts.
(c) For radio broadcasting license holders located in areas declared of provincial or municipal disaster, provided that the measure is necessary for the continuity of the service. In exceptional circumstances for justified economic or social reasons, the enforcement authority may agree to reduce up to 50% of the total amount of the tax for specified periods of no more than twelve months.
(d) Holders of licenses and/ or authorizations of open ACS whose delivery area is located in towns with less than 3,000 inhabitants.
(e) The stations of the national State, the provincial states, the municipalities, the national universities, the university institutes, the stations of the Native Peoples and those contemplated in Article 149 of this law.
(f) Establish a reduction of 20% of the tax for licensees of open ACS that meet the following conditions:
    (1) Possess only one license.
    (2) Have localities of up to 300,000 inhabitants assigned as the primary service provision area.
    (3) Have been awarded a category whose coverage area is up to 40 kilometers.
    (4) Have more than ten employees.
(g) Establish a reduction of 10% of the tax for licensees of ACS by subscription that meet the following conditions:
    (1) Possess only one license.
    (2) Have localities with up to 25,000 inhabitants assigned as the primary service provision area.
    (3) Have more than ten employees.

Chapter 2. Private Broadcasting

§1. Different Categories of Private Broadcasters

284. The PSBs are operated by three types of providers: (1) state-run, (2) privately managed for profit, and (3) privately run non-profit. The holders of this right are, respectively, entities subject to public law taking part of the state or non-state public law entities, corporations, and entities subject to private law, with or without profit goal (section 21).

285. The entities listed in (1) above which propose to install and operate a PSB must obtain the corresponding authorization from the enforcement authority under the conditions established by the regulations (section 22).

286. However, the rest of the entities shall obtain the corresponding license. Indeed, licenses will be awarded to entities privately managed for profit and privately run non-profit and to non-state public law entities insofar as it is not provided for in this law that an authorization is granted (section 23).

287. In order to guarantee the principles of diversity, plurality and respect for the local, human beings or legal entities may be holders or have participation in companies that hold licenses for PSB, subject to the following limits (section 45):

(1) In the national order:
  (a) One license for PSB on satellite support. The ownership of a license for satellite PSB by subscription excludes the possibility of being the holder of any other type of license for PSB under the Media Law and ICT services regulated by ICT Law.
  (b) Up to fifteen PSB licenses in the case of broadcast television broadcasting or sound broadcasting.
(2) In local order:
  (a) One AM sound broadcasting license.
  (b) One license for sound broadcasting by FM or up to two licenses when there are more than eight licenses in the primary service area.
  (c) One open television broadcasting license.

288. In no case may the total sum of licenses granted in the same primary service area or group of them that overlap in a majority way exceed the number of four licenses.

289. Licenses for direct broadcasting services by satellite and licenses for mobile broadcasting services will have as a condition of granting and continuity of their validity—each one of them—that they may not be accumulated with licenses for other services of a different kind or nature, except for the transmission of the existing open terrestrial television service prior to the transition processes to digitized services and the channel that will replace it from time to time (section 46).

290. Preserving the rights of license or authorization holders, the enforcement authority must submit a report to the National Executive Power and the National Congress Bicameral Commission on a biannual basis, analyzing the adequacy of the rules on multiple licenses and non-concurrency in order to optimize the use of the spectrum by the application of new technologies (section 47).

291. The enforcement authority will establish direct award mechanisms for very low power open PSB, the scope of which corresponds to the definitions provided in the technical service standard, as an exception, in circumstances of proven spectrum availability and in sites of high social vulnerability and/ or low demographic density and provided that their programming commitments are aimed at satisfying communicational demands of a social nature. These broadcasters may access a license extension upon expiration of the term, provided that the spectrum availability circumstances that gave rise to such award are maintained. Otherwise, the license will expire and the radioelectric location will be subject to a tender process. The relevant authority will not authorize in any case the increase of the effective radiated power or the change of location to the radio broadcasting stations whose license has been awarded by rule of this article (section 49).

§2. Licensing Requirements

292. Natural persons, such as holders of PSB licenses, as well as human beings as shareholders and/ or partners of legal entities for profit, must meet the following conditions at the time of their presentation to the process of awarding the license and maintain during their validity (section 24):

(a) Be born in Argentina or national by option or naturalized with a minimum residence of five years in the country.
(b) Be of legal age (over 18 years old) and legally capable.
(c) Not having been a de facto government official, in the positions and ranks established to date in Article 5, paragraph a) to paragraph o) and paragraphs q), r), s) and v) of Law 25,188 or those that in the future modify or replace it.
(d) Be able to demonstrate the origin of the funds committed to the investment to be made.
(e) Human beings as shareholders and/ or partners of profit legal entities and the members of the administration and control bodies of legal entities for non-profit purposes must prove the origin of the funds as long as they commit investments in a personal capacity.
(f) Not be incapacitated or disqualified, civilly or criminally, to contract or engage in business, nor have they been convicted of a fraudulent crime, of public action or private instance (requires final ruling not subject to appeal, Decree 1225/10).
(g) Not to be a debtor in default of tax, social security, union, social security or rights management entities, nor be a debtor of the tax and/ or fines established in this law.

(h) Not to be a judicial magistrate, legislator, public or military official or active security personnel. This condition will not be required in the case of mere members of a non-profit legal entity.
(i) Not to be a director or administrator of a legal entity or a shareholder who owns 10% or more of the shares that make up the corporate will of a legal person providing by license, concession, or permission of a national public service, provincial or municipal.

293. Legal entities as holders of PSB licenses and as shareholders and/ or partners of legal entities holders of PSB must meet the following terms at the time of their presentation to the process of awarding the license and maintain during its validity (section 25):

(a) Be a legally incorporated legal entity in the country. When the applicant is a legal entity in the process of incorporation, the awarding of the license will be conditional on its regular incorporation.
(b) Not having a corporate legal relationship or direct or indirect subjection to foreign PSB companies. In the case of non-profit legal entities, their directors and directors must not have direct or indirect ties with national or foreign PSB and telecommunications services of the commercial private sector. In order to comply with this requirement, it must be proven that the origin of the funds of the non-profit legal entities is not directly or indirectly linked to national or foreign companies of PSB and telecommunications services of the commercial private sector.
(c) They may not be affiliates or subsidiaries of foreign companies or carry out corporate acts, contracts or agreements that allow a controlling position of foreign capital in the management of the licensee legal entity.
The conditions established in paragraphs b) and c) will not be applicable when, according to international treaties to which the Nation is a party, effective reciprocity is established in the PSB activity.
(d) Not being the owner or shareholder who owns 10% or more of the shares or quotas that allow the shareholder to determine the corporate decisions—or its shareholder—of a public utility concessionaire granted a National, Provincial, or Municipal state. This restriction is not applicable in the case of non-profit legal entities (section 30).
(e) Legal persons may not issue shares, bonds, debentures, titles, or any type of negotiable obligations without the authorization of ENACOM when from these operations a percentage greater than 30% of the capital stock that attends the formation of corporate decisions (all issuance of shares, bonds, debentures, titles or any type of negotiable obligations or the constitution of trusts on its shares must have the authorization of ENACOM, prior to its realization; Decree 1225/10).
(f) Not be a debtor of tax, social security, union, social security or rights management entities, nor be a debtor of the lien and/ or fines established in this law (compliance with the tax, labor and social obligations must be proven by presenting a certificate of free debt issued by the respective collection entity; Decree 1225/10).

(g) To be able to demonstrate the origin of the funds committed to the investment to be made.

294. The requirements set forth above must be fulfilled by the companies with an ideal existence that enter—directly or indirectly—due to the transfer of shares or quotas of the licensees, in the cases authorized by the Media Law or by virtue of corporate reorganization processes (Decree 1225/10).

295. The profit and non-profit legal entities holders of PSB licenses, the members of its administration and control bodies organizations, its shareholder and/ or partners and/ or members of them, may not be awarded or participate under any title in the exploitation of PSB licenses when said participation directly or indirectly means exceeding the limit of licenses set forth by Article 45 of the Media Law (section 26). In order to properly control those limitations, the degrees of corporate control, as well as the degrees of direct and indirect corporate ties, must be fully disclosed (section 27). With the filing of a petition for a PSB license or for the authorization of transfer of shares or part quotas, the petitioning legal entity must prove the entirety of the corporate integration up to its last controlling party, detailing the share capital and the amount of shares or quotas that the partners have at each level (Decree 1225/10).

296. The enforcement authority must evaluate the proposals for the award of licenses considering the requirements of the Media Law and on the basis of roots and communicational proposal (the latter replaces the previous requirement of previous experience as a way to facilitate new entrant licensees). The other requirements that are set forth and detailed above are considered admissibility conditions (section 28).

297. When the service provider is a commercial company, it must have a capital stock of Argentina origin, allowing the participation of foreign capital up to a maximum of thirty percent (30%) of the share capital and granting the right to vote up to the same percentage of the thirty percent (30%) provided that this percentage does not mean directly or indirectly control of the licensee (section 29).

298. This restriction is in line with Law 25,750 (Official Gazette July 7, 2003) which further set forth that said percentage may be increased in reciprocity with the countries that contemplate foreign investment in their communication media regime, up to the percentage allow by it.

299. The following are not covered by these provisions (Law 25,750, section 2):

(a) The means of communication that on the date of entry into force of this law are owned or controlled by a foreign entity.
(b) The contracts for the assignment of shares, quotas or the transfer of ownership of the license entered into prior to the effective date of this law and which have not yet been approved by the competent bodies.

300. Non-profit entities holding a PSB license are allowed (section 30) to oversee public utilities (*servicios públicos*) as concessionaire, in which case they must comply with the following obligations:

(a) Set up a business unit for the purposes of providing the PSB and run it separately from the business unit of the public service in question.
(b) Keep a separate accounting and bill separately the benefits corresponding to the licensed PSB.
(c) Not to engage in anticompetitive practices such as tied practices and cross-subsidies with funds from the public service towards the licensed PSB (the ENACOM may order comprehensive audits in order to verify the absence of anticompetitive practices; Decree 1225/10).
(d) Provide—when requested—to competitors access to their own support infrastructure, especially poles, masts and ducts, under market conditions. In cases where there is no agreement between the parties, intervention must be requested from the enforcement authority (in the event of a conflict, the Antitrust Authority may be required to evaluate the circumstances of the case, with special attention to the modes of commercialization and stages of expansion of the network on own assets; Decree 1225/10).
(e) Not to engage in anticompetitive practices regarding the rights to display the content to be broadcast on their networks and facilitate a growing percentage to be determined by the authority applying to the distribution of content from independent third parties.

301. The comprehensive evaluation of the interest of the population will take into account factors such as the promotion and/ or dissemination of the local cultural environment, the benefits of the investment made in the area, the creation of sources of work in the locality of provision and all other circumstance where there is evidence of a benefit for the local community. The application submitted must be notified to the local operating licensees. In the event of opposition to a license application, copies of the file will be extracted and forwarded to the Antitrust Authority and its amendments to issue the opinion required by the Media Law. The presentation of oppositions will not imply the suspension of the procedure, but the administrative act of granting will be subject to the conditions of adjudication that are ruled as a result of the aforementioned referral.

302. In addition to the conditions and requirements established above, legal entities which are licensees of PSB must meet the following conditions (section 31):

(a) In the case of corporation in which stock is expressed in shares, the shares must be nominated, registered and not endorsable.

(b) The controlling and controlled companies will be considered the same person, in accordance with the provisions of Article 33 of the Commercial Companies Law 19,550.[47]

I. PSB Licences and Authorizations Awarding Regimen

303. The licenses corresponding to non-satellite PSB that use the radioelectric spectrum, contemplated by the Media Law, will be awarded through the open and permanent public tender regime (section 32).

304. Licenses for open PSBs whose primary service area exceeds 50 kilometers and which are located in towns of more than 500,000 inhabitants will be awarded after a tender by the National Executive Power. Those corresponding to the remaining open PSB and PSB that use non-satellite radio links and that are planned will be awarded by the enforcement authority. In all cases and prior to the award, a technical report from the competent bodies will be required (section 32).

305. For the calls, flexible technological criteria must be adopted allowing the optimization of the resource by application of new technologies in order to facilitate the incorporation of new participants in the activity (section 32).

306. The frequencies in which tender process requires a technical plan that is not awarded will remain in public, open and permanent tender process. The application authority shall call a new competition round when a new interested party file its motion for a license (section 32). When an interested party requests the opening of a contest, the call must be made within sixty calendar days of presenting the documentation and the formalities established by the regulations (section 32).

307. The inclusion in the technical plan of any radioelectric location which is included in a tender process may be requested at the request of the interested party. Should its feasibility and technical compatibility with the Technical Plan be verified, a tender must be called for its award (section 32).

308. Applications for the opening of public tenders for the award of PSB licenses that use radio spectrum must be submitted to the ENACOM which will establish at least two periods per year, during which the presentation of the respective applications will be admitted. The presentations made outside the term foreseen for each period will be considered present for the subsequent period. All public contests will be called and conducted by the ENACOM. When it corresponds that the license is issued by the National Executive Power, the ENACOM will send the proceedings with the respective draft decree and elevation note in order to complete

47. "Controlled companies are those in which another company, directly or through another company in turn controlled: 1) Has participation, by any title, that grants the necessary votes to form the corporate decisions in ordinary shareholding meetings; 2) Exercises a dominant influence as a result of shares, quotas or parts of interest owned, or because of the special links between the companies."

the processing and examination thereof prior to the issuance of the administrative awarding act. The ENACOM is empowered to decide on the characteristics of calls for public tenders by virtue of the availability of spectrum and the incorporation of new technologies (Decree 1225/10).

309. The incorporation of new radio locations in the Technical Frequency Plan will be carried out under the conditions set jointly by the ENACOM. The Authority will determine in which cases it will be admitted that the accreditation of the technical conditions of the stations is carried out through technical advice from the universities that work in the region in which the installation of the stations is planned. (Decree 1225/10).

310. Whoever has requested the opening of a public tender and notified of its call will not participate in it and may not require the opening of a public tender for a term of two years, counted from the last request (Decree 1225/10).

311. Public tenders for the granting of open PSB licenses awarded by the National Executive Power, and those corresponding to open PSB by subscription that use non-satellite radio links and that are planned, awarded by the ENACOM, which are the object of call from this regulation, must contemplate, prior to the call to the respective public tender, the population data established by the last National Population Census, prepared by the INDEC's (Decree 1225/10).

312. The requirements and application modalities for the opening of competitions and inclusion of frequencies in the Technical Plan will be established by the ENACOM (Decree 1225/10).

313. The terms and conditions for the award of licenses must be approved by the enforcement authority. The specifications will be prepared by considering differentiated characteristics, depending on whether they are specifications for the award of licenses to legal persons and whether they are for profit or not (section 33).

314. The criteria for evaluating license applications and proposals must follow the following criteria (section 34):

(a) The expansion or preservation of pluralism in the offer of PSB and in the set of information sources, considering the geographical coverage.
(b) The guarantees for the free and pluralistic expression of ideas and opinions in PSB which editorial and content responsibility will be assumed by the awardee (among other aspects, the proposal that tends to deconcentrate ownership of PSB should be taken into account favorably; transparency in the identity of the actual owners of the service; the formal and operational separation between the journalistic interests of those commercial, financial, private, governmental or of any other nature, and the respect and promotion of the plurality of voices; Decree 1225/10).

(c) Satisfaction of the interests and needs of potential users of the PSB, taking into account the geographical coverage, the characteristics of the service or the signals that would be broadcasted and, if part of the service is to be provided through paid access, the most beneficial relationship for the subscriber between the price and the services offered, as long as it does not jeopardize the viability of the service.
(d) The promotion, where appropriate, of the development of the "information society" that will provide the service by including related services, additional interactive services and other associated benefits.
(e) The provision of additional facilities to those legally required to ensure access to the service for people with disabilities or special needs.
(f) Contribution to the development of the content industry.
(g) The development of certain content of social interest.
(h) The criteria that, in addition, may set the specifications.

315. The patrimonial capacity will be evaluated in order to verify the admissibility and viability conditions of the proposal (section 35).

316. In each call for tender, the enforcement authority must insert the scoring grid to be used corresponding to the communication proposal evaluation, in accordance with the objectives set forth by the Media Law, as well as a scoring grid referring to the trajectory of human beings who are part of the project, in order to prioritize greater roots. Licensees must maintain the guidelines and objectives of the communication proposal expressed by the committed programming throughout the term of the license (section 36).

317. PSB license awarding to public legal entities, National Universities, Native Peoples and the Catholic Church is carried out on demand and directly, according to the availability of spectrum, when pertinent (section 37).

318. The granting of authorizations for persons of state and non-state public law, national universities, national university institutes, Native Peoples and the Catholic Church will be carried out at the request of the interested entity and directly, bearing in mind, when pertinent, the spectrum availability, the preexistence of services similar to those requested in the same or different coverage area and/ or the overlapping of frequencies in said location and the reserves provided for in Article 89 of the Media Law (Decree 1225/10).

319. Those interested in obtaining the authorization established in Article 22 of the Media Law must submit a communication proposal that responds to the objectives listed in Article 3 of the aforementioned law. This proposal must also contain, among other aspects, the requested coverage area, technical specifications, the corresponding programming plan and its form of financing, observing the provisions established in the Media Law and in these regulations. This proposal must be publicly accessible (Decree 1225/10).

320. At the time of requesting an authorization, the applicant must present a descriptive report of the technical and cultural project that certifies the conditions in which it intends to fulfill the objectives of the Media Law in terms of satisfaction of the right to freedom of expression, right to information and communication, as well as the values of diversity, pluralism, and the development of the information society (Decree 1225/10).

321. Notwithstanding that the assignment is made by means of authorization without prior competition, as a requirement of its origin, the sustainability of the project of the station to promote its infrastructure and its own production must be proved in the quotas established by the Media Law (Decree 1225/10).

322. ENACOM will award on demand the licenses for the installation and exploitation of PSB on satellite support. In this case, the granting of the license does not imply the award of orbital points (section 38).

323. Licenses will be granted for a period of ten years from the date of the resolution of the enforcement authority that authorizes the starting of regular broadcasts (section 39).

324. The licenses will be subject to a first extension for five years, which will be automatic and to which the licensee will be entitled upon the mere prior request to ENACOM. Said request must be made, under penalty of expiration of the right, within the period between twelve months and six months prior to the expiration date of the license. Exceptionally and with prior technical opinion, even before the expiration of the license, ENACOM may summon the licensee and propose a technological update within the terms and conditions determined by the relevant authority (section 40).

325. Subsequent extensions will be for ten years and will be granted by ENACOM; however, the relevant authority may call new licensees to tender under the terms of Article 32 of the Media Law based on reasons of public interest, the introduction of new technologies or compliance with international agreements. In this case, the previous licensees will not have any acquired rights regarding their license (section 40).

326. The extension request must comply with the requirements and procedure established by the ENACOM regulations and the following conditions (section 40):

(a) The request shall be made to ENACOM within the period between twelve months and six months prior to the expiration date of the license, under penalty of expiration of the right.
(b) At the time of submitting the request for an extension of ten years, the licensee must prove: (i) That it meets the conditions required by current regulations to be the holder of PSB licenses; (ii) That it has fulfilled all the obligations derived from its license; (iii) That it does not have any debt for national taxes or for the social security obligations under his charge.

327. The authorizations will be granted indefinitely (section 40).

328. The PSB licenses and the stakes of the licensees are only transferable to those persons who meet the admissibility conditions established for their award (section 41). Those transfers will be considered made in ad referendum of ENACOM approval and must be communicated within thirty days after their completion. If ENACOM has not expressly rejected the transfer within ninety days as from the date in which the relevant ENACOM area considers properly fulfilled the communication (ENACOM Resolution 18/2016, Official Gazette March 9, 2016), it will be understood tacitly approved, and the interested party may request the registration in its name. If there are observations, the referred period will be counted as from when they have been considered fulfilled (section 41).

329. The license extension request must be made within a minimum period of eighteen months and a maximum period of thirty-six months prior to their expiration date, without exception. On this occasion, the licensee must prove that he maintains all the conditions required by the Media Law in the personal, corporate, patrimonial and background aspects of the applicant and that he has not been repeatedly sanctioned with serious misconduct. Likewise, the necessary documentation will be required to verify compliance with the programming percentages required by law in relation to content, depending on the type in question (Decree 1225/10).

330. The applicant for the extension must submit: (1) report that synthesizes the performance carried out since obtaining the license; (2) proposal of programming appropriate to the experience of the operation on whose service the license extension is requested. In the event that the evaluations carried out in the foregoing aspects are approved, the public hearing procedure will begin. The procedures for the extension of the license of ACS whose service area is localities of less than 30,000 inhabitants may be exempted from the public hearing process, provided that no registration is registered in the registry of interested parties whose opening has for this purpose the Enforcement Authority. The Enforcement Authority will establish the other conditions for the convocation and development of public hearings (Decree 1225/10).

331. The Enforcement Authority must decide on the issuance of the extension within 180 business days from the holding of the public hearing, a period during which it must verify the continuity of the award conditions of the license by the applicant and their partners or members. If applicable, reports may be requested from the Antitrust Law Enforcement Authority. The public hearing will be held under the conditions of holding established in the applicable general regime (Decree 1225/10).

332. The execution of the transfer contract without the corresponding approval, express or tacit, will be sanctioned with the expiration of the license awarded, with prior notice from ENACOM (section 41). The Enforcement Authority may authorize transfers of shares or part quotas in proportions greater than those established in Article 41 of the Media Law only when the original holders are affected by the assumptions provided for in Articles 51 and 52 of the aforementioned law. Registration made in breach of the provisions of this article will be void without prejudice to the sanctions that may correspond to the official who authorizes it (Decree 1225/10). Licenses granted to privately managed non-profit providers are nontransferable (section 41).

333. Both the PSB licenses and the PSB authorizations are not sizable by creditors and no more rights can be established on them than those expressly contemplated in the Media Law (section 42).

334. The exploitation of PSB license or authorization will be carried out by its holder. It will be considered a delegation of exploitation and configures a serious fault (section 44):

(a) Assign under whichever legal way or simple sale of programming spaces in favor of third parties, in whole or in part.
(b) Enter into exclusive contracts with advertising marketing companies (It is understood that there will be exclusivity when at least 60% of the advertising spaces from private sources are hired by a natural or legal person other than the licensee, permit holder or an authorized person, Decree 1225/10).
(c) Enter into exclusive contracts with content-producing organizations (it is understood that exclusivity will exist when more than 30% of the programming and/or broadcast spaces are hired by a natural or legal person other than the licensee, permit holder or an authorized person pursuant to Decree 1225/10).
(d) Grant power of attorney to third parties or carry out legal businesses that imply the partial or full substitution of the PSB license or authorization holder (it will be considered that there is a legal business that allows the substitution of the owners of the exploitation when goods assigned to the service are replaced by third-party goods. This assumption will not be configured when the substitution is authorized by the relevant authority—and the licensee proves that he possesses sufficient title over the assets for their use, Decree 1225/10).

335. The licenses will expire (section 50):

(a) Due to the expiration of its term without the extension having been requested.
(b) Due to the death of the human being licensed, except for the case in which her/his heirs decided to carry on the license.
(c) Due to the incapacity of the human being licensed.
(d) Due to the failure to restructure the legal entity shareholding in case of death meeting the criteria considered under the granted license.
(e) By renouncing to the license.
(f) By declaration of expiration.
(g) Due to bankruptcy of the licensee.
(h) Due to not regularly starting the PSB within the term set by the competent authority.

(i) Due to loss or noncompliance with the requirements for the award established herein, after compliance with the summary with a guarantee of the right of defense.
(j) Due to unjustified suspension of emissions for more than fifteen days within a period of one year.

336. In the event of termination of the license for any of the abovementioned causes, the enforcement authority may order transitory measures that ensure the continuity of the service until its normalization in order to safeguard the public and social interest. Once a license has been extinguished under the terms of Article 50 of the Media Law, the dismantling of the infrastructure is prohibited until the Enforcement Authority issues express authorization in this regard (Decree 1225/ 10).

337. The shares of the PSB licenses may be traded on the stock market for a maximum total of 45% of the share capital with voting rights (section 54). Prior authorization must be required from the enforcement authority for the constitution of trusts on the shares of licensee legal entities when they are not traded in the stock market in the case third parties are granted rights to participate in the formation of the decision of the legal entity (section 55).

II. Medial Law Registers

338. The shareholders' ledger of legal entities must allow the verification at all times of compliance with the provisions relating to the ownership of the shareholding and the conditions of the shareholders. Failure to comply with this provision will constitute a serious offense (section 56).

339. The PSB relevant authority will keep updated and freely accessible to the public, the Public Registry of PSB Licenses and Authorizations that must contain the data that allow identifying the licensee or authorized entities, their shareholders, members of the administration and control bodies, technical parameters, dates of start and expiration of licenses and extensions, sanctions and other data that are of interest to ensure transparency. The enforcement authority must establish a public consultation mechanism via the Internet (section 57).

340. The PSB relevant authority will keep the Public Registry of Signals and Production Companies updated on a public basis, including:

(a) Producers of media content to be distributed via PSB for the sole purpose of verifying compliance with production quotas.
(b) Companies that generate and/ or commercialize signals or exhibition rights for the distribution of content and programs via PSB.

341. The regulations will determine the registration data to be completed by them and which data must be publicly accessible, and the enforcement authority must establish a public consultation mechanism via the Internet (section 58).

342. The PSB relevant authority will keep the Public Registry of Advertising Agencies and Advertising Producers, whose registration will be mandatory for the commercialization of spaces in broadcasting services. The regulations will determine which registration data must be completed by them and which ones must be public. The record will include:

(a) Advertising agencies that advertise via PSB.
(b) Brokers that mediate in the commercialization of advertising via PSB.

343. The enforcement authority must keep the registry of licenses and authorizations updated and establish a public consultation mechanism via the Internet (section 59).

344. The PSB licensees and/ or authorized may not distribute advertising of any kind from advertising agencies or advertising producers that have not complied with the provisions of the abovementioned registry (section 61).

345. Those responsible for the production and emission of packaged programmes—“signals” (*señales*) —that are broadcast in the national territory must comply with the following requirements:

(a) Register in the abovementioned registry.
(b) Appoint a legal representative or agency with sufficient powers.
(c) Establish legal domicile in the Autonomous City of Buenos Aires.

346. Failure to comply with the provisions will be considered a serious offense, as well as the distribution or retransmission of the signals for those who did so without proof. The PSB licensees and/ or authorized may not broadcast or retransmit signals generated abroad that do not meet the aforementioned requirements (section 60).

III. PSB Licensees and Authorized Obligations

347. Holders of PSB licenses and PSB authorizations must observe, in addition to the established obligations, the following (section 72):

(a) Provide all the information and collaboration that the enforcement authority requires and that is considered necessary or convenient for the proper fulfillment of the functions that correspond to them.

(b) Provide free of charge to the enforcement authority the monitoring service of its emissions in the technical form and in the places determined by the regulatory norms.
(c) Register or record the broadcasts, keeping them for the term and under the conditions established by the enforcement authority.
(d) Maintain a file of the broadcast production whose contents must be available for public protection. To such ends, the broadcasters must send the contents that are required to the General Archive of the Nation. Commercial use of these files is prohibited.
(e) Each licensee or authorized person must make available, as easily accessible information, a public access folder to which its exhibition on digital support on the internet must be added. It must include:
  (i) The license or authorization holders.
  (ii) Programming commitments that justified obtaining the license, if applicable.
  (iii) Members of the governing body.
  (iv) Technical specifications authorized in the act of granting the license or authorization.
  (v) Evidence of the number of programs for children's programming, of public interest, of educational interest.
  (vi) The information regularly sent to the enforcement authority in compliance with the law.
  (vii) The sanctions that the licensee or authorized person may have received.
  (viii) The official advertising guideline (s) received by the licensee from all national, provincial, municipal jurisdictions and from the Autonomous City of Buenos Aires, detailing each one of them.
(f) Include a warning in the case of previously recorded content in news programs or with public participation.
(g) Make available to the public at least once per broadcast day through overprinting devices in audiovisual media the identification and address of the license or authorization holder (section 72).

IV. Technical Regulation of PSB

348. The PSB license holders and PSB authorization holders must comply with the technical requirements established within a period of no more than 180 calendar days from the award or authorization. Once the requirements have been met, ENACOM, together with the relevant technical authority, will proceed to technically enable the facilities and issue the resolution for the regular start of the service. Until the administrative act is issued authorizing the start of regular broadcasts, there will be a test and adjustment of technical parameters; therefore, the dissemination of advertising is prohibited (section 84).

349. The PSB license holders, authorization holders and the holders of signal registration must ensure the regularity and continuity of the transmissions and compliance with the programming schedules, which must be communicated to the ENACOM (section 85).

350. Licensees of open PSB and holders of PSB by subscription in their own signal must adjust their transmission continuously and permanently to the following minimum times per day (section 86):

	Radio (Hours)	*TV (Hours)*
Primary service area of 600,000 or more inhabitants	16	14
Primary service area with between 100,000 and 600,000 inhabitants	14	10
Primary service area with between 30,000 and 100,000 inhabitants	12	8
Primary service area with between 3,000 and 30,000 inhabitants	12	6
Primary service area of less than 3,000 inhabitants	10	6

V. Technical Regulation of PSB

351. Open PSBs and/ or that use radio spectrum will be installed and operated subject to the technical parameters and quality of service established by the National Service Standard established by the enforcement authority and other bodies with jurisdiction in the matter. The technical equipment and civil works of its facilities will be adjusted to the technical project presented (section 87).

352. The ENACOM will prepare and modify, with the participation of the respective technical authority, the National Service Standard subject to the following criteria (section 88):

(a) The technical norms and restrictions that arise from the international treaties in force in which the Argentine Nation takes part.
(b) The requirements of the national communication policy and of the municipal and provincial jurisdictions.
(c) The use of the radioelectric spectrum that promotes the largest number of stations.
(d) The geomorphological conditions of the area that will be determined as the service area.

353. Any radio location not provided for in the standard may be awarded at the request of the interested party, according to the corresponding procedure, if its feasibility and radio compatibility with the locations provided for in the National Service Standard are verified.

354. The Technical Plan of Frequencies and the Technical Service Standards will be considered the object of positive information and must be available on the website of the relevant authority (section 88). At the time of preparing the Technical Plan for Frequencies, the relevant federal authority must make the following frequency reservations without prejudice to the possibility of expanding frequency reservations by virtue of the incorporation of new technologies that allow greater use of the radioelectric spectrum (section 89):

(a) For the national State, the necessary frequencies will be reserved for the fulfillment of the objectives of RTA S.E., its operational repeaters, and the repeaters necessary to cover the entire national territory.
(b) For each provincial State and the Autonomous City of Buenos Aires, 1 AM sound broadcasting frequency, 1 FM sound broadcasting frequency and 1 open television frequency, with more than the necessary repeaters in order to cover its entire territory.
(c) For each municipal State, 1 frequency of sound broadcasting frequency by FM.
(d) In each location where the headquarters of a national university is located, 1 frequency for open television and 1 frequency for radio broadcasting stations. The enforcement authority may authorize by means of a founded resolution the operation of additional frequencies for educational, scientific, cultural or research purposes requested by national universities.
(e) 1 AM frequency, 1 FM frequency and 1 television frequency for the Native Peoples in the localities where each town is settled.
(f) Thirty-three percent of the planned radioelectric locations, in all terrestrial sound and television broadcasting bands, in all coverage areas for people with an ideal non-profit existence.

355. The frequency reservations established in this article cannot be waived. The federal relevant authority will allocate the frequencies recovered by extinction, license, or authorization expiration, or by reassignment of bands due to technological standard migration, to the satisfaction of the reservations stated in this article, especially those contemplated in subparagraphs e) and f) (section 89).

356. The enforcement authority, by application of the National Service Standard, together with the regulatory authority and the enforcement authority in the field of Telecommunications, may vary the technical parameters of the broadcasting stations, without affecting the conditions of competition in the area of coverage of the license, either generating any type of indemnification or compensation right for its holders. In the notification communicating the modification of the technical parameter, the term granted will be determined, which in no case will be less than 180 calendar days (section 90).

357. The transport of point-to-point signals between their provider and the licensee, within the framework of the corresponding technical and regulatory standards, is subject to the agreement of the parties (section 91).

VI. New Technologies and Services

358. The incorporation of new technologies and services that are not operational as of the effective date of the Media Law will be determined by the national Executive Power according to the following guidelines (section 92):

(a) Harmonization of the use of the radioelectric spectrum and technical standards with the member countries of Mercosur and Region II of the International Telecommunications Union (ITU).
(b) The determination of new segments of the radioelectric spectrum and of technical standards that ensure sufficient capacity for the location or relocation of all installed radio broadcasters, ensuring that the introduction of technology favors plurality and the entry of new operators. It will grant licenses under equitable and nondiscriminatory conditions.
(c) The relevant authority for PSB may, with the intervention of the technical authority, authorize experimental broadcasts for research and development of technological innovations, which will not generate rights and for which the respective permission will be granted. The assigned frequencies will be subject to immediate return at the request of the enforcement authority.
(d) The relocation of broadcasters may not affect the conditions of competition in the area of coverage of the license, without prejudice to the incorporation of new actors in the activity according to paragraph b) above.
(e) The possibility of granting new licenses to new operators to provide services under conditions of open access or in a combined or hybrid mode simultaneously with open services or with subscription services.

359. In the case of the presence of dominant positions in the existing services market, the enforcement authority must give preference in the exploitation of new services and markets to new participants in said activities (section 92).

VII. Transition to Digital Services

360. In the transition to digital broadcasting services, the rights and obligations of licensees obtained by public tender for analogical (as opposed to digital services) open services must be maintained, guaranteeing their validity and coverage area, under the conditions established by the National Plan for Digital PSB, if they are in operation until the date established by the national Executive Power according to the third paragraph of this article. It is established that during the period in which the licensee broadcasts simultaneously in an analogic and digital way, and provided that the content is the same, the additional signal will not be computed for the purposes of calculating the limits provided in the clause of multiplicity of licenses of the Media Law, section 45 (section 93).

361. The broadcasting conditions during the transition will be regulated by means of the National Plan for Digital PSB, which will be approved by the National Executive Power within 180 days of the entry into force of the Media Law. The National Executive Power will set the date of completion of the technological transition process for each service. Said plan must foresee that the licensees or authorized ones that operate digital fixed or mobile non-satellite services must reserve a portion of the total transport capacity of the assigned radioelectric channel for the emission of contents defined as of "universal scope" by the regulation to dictate by the national Executive Power. Likewise, it must foresee the transition conditions of state-owned, university, Indigenous Peoples and Catholic Church broadcasting stations (section 93).

362. In order to guarantee citizen participation, the universalization of access to new technologies and the satisfaction of the objectives set forth in the Media Law, prior to any decision-making, a procedure for the participatory elaboration of norms and another of public hearings, according to the pertinent norms and principles. Once the transition process to digital services is completed under the conditions established after fulfilling the obligations set forth previously, the frequency bands originally assigned to licensees and authorized for analogical services will be available to be assigned by the Power National Executive for the fulfillment of the objectives set in the Media Law, subsection e) of section 3 (section 93).

363. To this end, future regulatory and technical service standards should tend to the ordering of the radioelectric spectrum in accordance with the guidelines established by international bodies for the use of the digital dividend after the completion of the migration processes to the new services. In order to guarantee citizen participation, the universalization of access to new technologies and the satisfaction of the objectives set forth in the Media Law, prior to any decision-making, a procedure for the participatory elaboration of norms and another of public hearings, according to the pertinent norms and principles (section 93).

364. Through Decree No. 1148/2009 (Official Gazette January 9, 2009), the Argentine Digital Terrestrial Television System (SATVD-T) was created based on the standard called ISDB-T (Integrated Services Digital Broadcasting Terrestrial), which consists of a set of technological patterns to be adopted for the transmission and reception of digital terrestrial signals, broadcasting of images and sound, and a term of ten years was established in order to carry out the transition process of analogical television to said system.

365. Resolution 1047/2014 (Official Gazette September 18, 2014), issued by the "AFSCA" approved the National Service Standard for the Audiovisual Communication Service for the open digital terrestrial television.

366. For the open digital terrestrial television service, the segment of the UHF frequency band between 470 and 608 MHz will be used, that is, between channels 14 and 36. The segment of the UHF frequency band between 470 and 512 MHz, channels 14 to 20, will be used when the Table of Attribution of Frequency Bands of the Argentine Republic allows it and electromagnetic compatibility with fixed and mobile services is verified. Restrictions derived from spectrum use agreements signed with neighboring countries will be taken into account (Article 6, Res. 1047/2014).

367. The number of digital channels of each radioelectric channel will be the result of multiplexing, which must be carried out according to the implementation schemes established by the corresponding authority. Said schemes will depend on the formats of the services considered, the application of radioelectric spectrum optimization criteria, and the incorporation of new providers. The formats referred to in this article will respond to the parameters indicated below or others that the corresponding authority defines in relation to each service (Article 7, Res. 1047/2014):

Format of Service	*Minimal Binary Transmission Rate (Mbit/s)*	*Maximum Binary Transmission Rate (Mbit/s)*
SD 576i/p	3	4, 5
HD 720p	6	9
Full HD 1080i	10	12

Chapter 3. Programme Standards

§1. Promotion of Diversity and Regional Content

368. The radio broadcasting stations that are members of a PSB network may not initiate simultaneous transmissions until the relevant PSB authority has issued the authorization of the corresponding agreement or contract for the creation of the network. The authority will have sixty business days to issue the request. In case of silence of the administration, authorization will be considered granted if the presentation contains all the required elements. Radio and/ or television networks may not be established between licensees with the same service area, except in the case of cities with up to 50,000 inhabitants, provided that it is a matter of retransmission of local content (section 62).

369. The constitution of radio and television networks is allowed, provided that they include a time limit, according to the following guidelines (section 63):

(a) The station adhered to one or more networks and may not cover more than 30% of its monthly broadcasts with these programmings in the case of stations located in cities with more than 1,500,000 inhabitants. When they are in cities with more than 600,000 inhabitants, this programming should not cover more than 40% of their monthly emissions and no more than 50% of their monthly emissions in other cities with inhabitants.
Those restrictions are not applicable to PSB rendered by national and provincial States, national universities and Native Peoples (section 64).
(b) The adhered station must maintain 100% of the contracting rights on the advertising broadcast in the programming in question.
(c) It must maintain the broadcast of a local news signal at central hours.

370. Providers of various types and classes of services may reciprocally agree on the conditions of retransmission of certain programs, provided that this retransmission of programs does not exceed 10% of the monthly broadcasts.

371. For the transmission of events of relevant interest, the constitution of open radio and television networks is allowed without limitations (section 63).

372. The Enforcement Authority will determine the limit on the number of network hours, in each case, for which it will ensure that the number of programming hours to be preserved to be broadcast from origin by each station, including sixty minutes in the Central Schedule, in addition to your own information service. Central Schedule is understood to be the time band from 7:00 p.m. to 11:00 p.m. for television and from 7:00 a.m. to 10:00 a.m. and from 7:00 p.m. to 10:00 p.m. for sound broadcasting. Multiple headers will exist when at least three stations of the proposed network do not own more than 60% of the rights of the programming that links them. Events of relevant interest will be those defined by the Enforcement

Authority by application of Article 15 of the Media Law. The events that are newsworthy and do not happen in a habitual or foreseeable way are exempted from the processing of the definition or qualification as such (Decree 1225/10).

§2. Programs Content Requirements

373. Holders of PSB licenses and/ or PSB authorizations must comply with the following guidelines regarding the content of their daily programming (section 65):

(1) Sound broadcasting services:
  (a) Private and non-state:
    (i) They must emit a minimum of 70% of national production.
    (ii) At least 30% of the broadcasted music must be of national origin, whether by national authors or interpreters, for each half-day of transmission. This quota of national music must be distributed proportionally throughout the programming and must also ensure the broadcast of 50% of music produced independently where the author and/ or interpreter exercises the marketing rights of their own songs, entitled to freely exploit and commercialize them. The PSB relevant authority may exempt radio broadcasting stations dedicated to foreign communities or thematic stations from this obligation.
    (iii) They must broadcast a minimum of 50% of their own production that includes local newscasts or news.
  (b) Broadcasters owned by provincial states, the Autonomous City of Buenos Aires, municipalities and national universities:
    (i) They must broadcast a minimum of 60% of local and own production, which includes local newscasts or news.
    (ii) They must broadcast a minimum of 20% of the total programming, programmes with educational, cultural and public interest content.

(2) Open television broadcasting services (section 65):
  (a) They must emit a minimum of 60% of national production.
  (b) They must broadcast a minimum of 30% of their own production, including local news. Without prejudice to the programming freedom of the PSB provider and the actual duration of the newscast services for the purposes of calculating local production, the allocation of such informative spaces to that minimum percentage of own production may not exceed 50% of that subtotal, considered for each half-day of broadcast, in order to promote other types of content or program productions. Thematic channels will be exempted from this obligation (Decree 1225/10).
  (c) They must emit a minimum of 30% of independent local production in the case of stations located in cities with more than 1,500,000 inhabitants. When they are located in towns with more than 600,000 inhabitants, they must emit a minimum of 15% of independent local production and a minimum of 10% in other locations.

(3) Fixed-reception subscription television services (section 65):

(a) They must include without coding the broadcasts and signals of Radio Televisión Argentina (State-owned), all the stations and public signals of the national State and in all those in which the national State has participation.
(b) They must order their programming grid in such a way that all the signals corresponding to the same genre are located in a correlative manner and order their presentation in the grid according to the regulations issued for this purpose, giving priority to local, regional and national signals.

Subscription television services must order their programming grid in such a way that all signals corresponding to the same genre are located in a correlative manner. The programming grid must give priority to local, regional and national signals and to those signals intended for children's, educational and informational programs (Decree 1225/10).

The programming grids of the subscription television systems must respect the regulations established for this purpose by the Enforcement Authority, which will include the signals registered in the Public Registry of Signals and Producers in the genre "Journalistic/ News." If there is no retransmission agreement for economic reasons between the owner of any of the "Journalistic/ News" signals and the owner of the PSB, the latter may not excuse himself from retransmitting the signal if it is delivered by its owner without post (Decree 1225/10).

The Enforcement Authority is competent to modify or update the ordering regime of the programming grid and to authorize the deviation of the provisions contained therein, if reasons of force majeure that require it are accredited (Decree 1225/10).

(c) Non-satellite subscription television services must include at least one signal of its own local production that satisfies the same conditions that this law establishes for open television broadcasts for each license or jurisdictional area that authorizes the laying. In the case of services located in cities with less than 6,000 inhabitants, the service may be offered by a regional signal.
(d) Non-satellite subscription television services must include, without coding, the broadcasts of the original open television services whose coverage area coincides with their service provision area.
(e) Non-satellite subscription television services must include, without coding, the signals generated by the provincial states, the Autonomous City of Buenos Aires and municipalities and national universities that are located in their service provision area.
(f) Satellite subscription television services must include, without coding, the open signals generated by the provincial states, by the Autonomous City of Buenos Aires and municipalities, and by national universities.
(g) Satellite subscription television services must include at least one signal of its own national production that satisfies the same conditions that this law establishes for open television broadcasts.
(h) Subscription television services must include in their channel grid a minimum of signals originating in MERCOSUR countries and in Latin American countries with which the Argentine Republic has signed or will sign

agreements for this purpose in the future and which must be registered in the registration of signals provided for in this law.

The national Executive Power will establish the pertinent conditions in the matter object of this article for the mobile television service, subject to their ratification by the Bicameral Commission provided for in the Media Law (section 65).

374. Open PSB must incorporate additional visual communication aids, such as sign language and audio descriptions, into locally produced signals in subscription systems. This requirement applies to informative, educational, cultural, and general interest programs of national production. The goal is to ensure accessibility for people with hearing disabilities, older adults, and anyone else who may have difficulty accessing the content. The regulation will determine the progressive conditions of its implementation (section 66).

375. PSB that broadcast television signals must meet the following screen quota (section 67):

- The licensees of open television services must exhibit in television premiere in their respective coverage areas, and per calendar year, eight national feature films, being able to choose to include up to three national telefilms in the same quantity, in both cases mainly produced by national independent production companies, whose broadcasting rights had been acquired prior to the start of filming.
- All licensees of subscription television services in the country and licensees of open television services whose total coverage area comprises less than 20% of the country's population may choose to meet the screen quota by acquiring, prior to filming, broadcasting rights to national films and telefilms produced by national independent production companies, for the value of 0.50% of the gross annual turnover of the previous year.
- The signals that are not considered national, authorized to be retransmitted by subscription television services, which broadcast fiction programs in a total of more than 50% of their daily programming, must allocate the value of 0.50% of the annual gross billing of the year prior to the acquisition, prior to the start of filming, of national film antenna rights.

§3. Protection of Minors (Indecency and Violence)

376. In all cases, the contents of the programming, its advances and advertising must comply with the following conditions (section 68):

(a) From 6:00 a.m. to 10:00 p.m., they must be suitable for all audiences.
(b) From 10 p.m. to 6 a.m., programs considered suitable for the elderly may be broadcast.

377. At the beginning of the programs that are not suitable for all audiences, the qualification that it deserves must be issued according to the categories described herein. During the first thirty seconds of each block, the symbol determined by the enforcement authority must be displayed in order to enable visual identification of the corresponding rating. In the event that the official time is not uniform throughout the territory of the Republic, the enforcement authority will modify the protection schedule for minors established in this article in order to unify its validity throughout the country.

378. Children under the age of 12 will not be allowed to participate in programs that are broadcast between 10 p.m. and 8 a.m., unless they have been recorded outside of those hours, a circumstance that must be mentioned in their broadcast.

379. The regulations will determine the existence of a minimum number of hours of production and transmission of specific audiovisual material for boys and girls in all open television channels whose origin is at least 50% of national production and will establish the conditions for the insertion of an explicit prior warning when, due to the need to provide information to the audience (newscasts/flashes), the principles of protection of minors may be violated at times not reserved for an adult audience (section 68).

380. The educational objectives set forth in the Media Law (sections 3, 4 and 68) consider the "Convention on the Rights of the Child" of constitutional hierarchy in accordance with Article 75, paragraph 22 of the National Constitution. The Convention, approved by our country through law 23,849.

§4. Human Dignity

381. The programming of the services provided for in this law must avoid content that promotes or incites discriminatory treatment based on race, color, sex, sexual orientation, language, religion, political opinions or of any other nature, origin, national or social status, economic position, birth, physical appearance, the presence of disabilities or that undermine human dignity or induce behaviors that are harmful to the environment or the health of people and the integrity of children or adolescents (section 70).

Chapter 4. Political Broadcasting

§1. Rules on Political Independence of Broadcasters

382. Argentine law has not regulations about political independence of broadcasters. Freedom of speech general framework shall be applicable to this.

§2. Fair Representation in Election Periods

383. The PSB licensees will be obliged to comply with the requirements established in the matter of political advertising and assign spaces in their programming to political parties during electoral campaigns in accordance with the provisions of the electoral law. Said spaces may not be subject to subdivisions or new assignments (section 74).

384. The process through which the electoral advertising regime in ACS is put into practice depends on the following:

- The execution and allocation of electoral advertising spaces through a Public Draw.
- The sending by the ENACOM of the lists of PSBs authorized to broadcast electoral advertising.
- The development of a computer platform (currently the Electoral Campaign Administration System—SACE) where political groups manage the assigned spaces on radio and television.

385. The ACSs affected the broadcast of electoral publicity during an electoral campaign:

- They are those broadcasting stations of open TV, cable TV, National Signals, AM and FM radios authorized by ENACOM.
- They must assign 5% of twelve hours of transmission (2,160 seconds per day) free of charge.

386. The percentages for each category are as follows:

- For presidential elections:
  - Fifty percent President/Vice President.
  - Twenty-five percent National Senators.
  - Twenty-five percent National Deputies.
- For legislative elections:
  - Fifty percent National Senators.
  - Fifty percent National Deputies.

387. In case a province holds its elections simultaneously and expressly adheres to the regime:

- For presidential elections:
  - Forty percent President/Vice President.
  - Fifteen percent National Senators.
  - Fifteen percent National Deputies.
  - Twenty percent Governor and Vice Governor.
  - Ten percent Provincial legislators.
- For legislative elections:
  - Forty percent National Senators.
  - Forty percent National Deputies.
  - Twenty percent Provincial legislators.

388. Likewise, the 2,160 seconds per day per ACS are distributed among all those political groupings (PA) that officialize lists of candidates as follows:

- Fifty percent equally among all PAs.
- Fifty percent in proportion to the votes obtained by the PA in the last election for the category of deputies.

389. The time given up by the ACSs is divided into four time slots:

- F1: 07:00 to 11:00 am.
- F2: 11:00 to 16:00 hs.
- F3: 16:00 to 20:00 hs.
- F4: 20:00 to 01:00 hs.

390. This time is expressed in modules, which means that:

- One module in TV = Twelve seconds.
- One module in radio = Nine seconds.

§3. News and Current Affairs Programmes

391. News and current affairs programmes are under the scope of the general media legislation, without a special regime described in Chapter 1 above.

§4. Political Advertising

392. The National Executive Power and the provincial executive powers may, in serious, exceptional, or institutional transcendence situations, order the integration of the national or provincial broadcasting chain which will be mandatory for all licensees (Media Law 26,522, section 75).

393. The ENACOM may order the issuance of messages of public interest. Broadcasting license holders must broadcast, free of charge, these messages according to the determined hourly frequency and in accordance with the regulations. The messages declared of public interest may not have a duration greater than 120 seconds and will not be counted in the advertising broadcast time limits determined in section 82 of the Media Law. For subscription services, this obligation will refer only to the signal of the company's own production (section 76). Said obligation will not apply when the messages are part of official advertising campaigns to which budgetary funds are applied to sustain them or are disseminated in other social communication media to which public funds are applied to sustain them. This time will not be computed for the purposes of the maximum advertising allowed by the Media Law.

394. The enforcement authority will provide, after consulting the Federal Council for Audiovisual Communication Services, the official advertising limits that private commercial or non-profit services may receive, considering the socioeconomic, demographic and market conditions of the different locations. For official advertising investment, the State must consider criteria of fairness and reasonableness in its distribution, considering the communicational objectives of the message in question (Media Law 26,522, section 76).

395. In Argentina, official advertising is any form of communication, advertisement or institutional campaign of an onerous, free or legally assigned nature carried out through any means of communication by the agencies listed in Article 8 of Law 24,156, the Banco de la Nación Argentina and its related companies, to disseminate actions or information of public interest. The relevant regulations are provided for in Law 24,156, its regulatory Decree 1344 of October 4, 2007, Decrees 357 of February 21, 2002; 151 of December 17, 2015 and 725 of May 31, 2016; Decree 984 of July 27, 2009, its regulation No. 14 of January 11, 2011, and Resolutions 247/2016 and 617-E/2016. The purpose of official advertising is to communicate measures, programs and information of public interest arising from the management of the national government.

396. However, as referred to above, there are emergency campaigns that may only be motivated by the presence of a natural catastrophe, threats to public health, safety or the environment, and alterations to social order or the normal functioning of public services in any area of the country. In these cases, the advertiser is the National Public Sector, which, according to Article 8 of Law 24,156, is comprised of:

- National Administration, comprising the Central Administration and the Decentralized Agencies, the latter including the Social Security Institutions.
- State Enterprises and Corporations, which includes State Enterprises, State Corporations, Corporations with majority State participation, Mixed Economy Corporations and all other business organizations in which the State has a majority participation in the capital or in the formation of corporate decisions.

- Public Entities expressly excluded from the National Administration, which covers any non-corporate state agency with financial autarchy, legal personality, and its own assets, where the national state has majority control of the assets or of the formation of decisions, including those non-state public entities where the national state has control of decisions.

397. Official advertising allocations are assigned to the different publications and/or media per campaign and using the following objective criteria:

- Scope of the media: Based on its circulation or audience, the determination of which the reference indicators in each market and the records that the supplier certifies by means of a sworn statement will be taken into account.
- Relevance of the message: Based on its specialization in relation to the target audience or public of the message.
- Geographic area: Based on the fact that they have a verifiable coverage of a certain geographic area or region in which the target audience or public of the message is circumscribed.
- Promotion of federalism and plurality of voices: Based on the fact that they are managed by non-profit social organizations that duly prove their social purpose, that broadcast in the languages of native peoples and/or that broadcast in low power categories according to the technical definitions established by ENACOM.
- In no case may any of the criteria exceed 60% of the total weighting for each campaign.

398. The following messages are excluded from official advertising:

- Any message or announcement that affects the rights enshrined in the treaties and declarations on human and social rights incorporated in the National Constitution.
- Any message that promotes particular interests of government officials or any political party.
- Any message or advertisement that, directly or indirectly, makes reference to the electoral campaign of the political party or parties participating in the government, whether at the National, Provincial or Municipal level, taking as a reference the electoral schedule and the candidates registered before the electoral authority.
- The use of official advertising to promote smear campaigns against individuals, institutions or civil society organizations.
- The promotion or dissemination that favors, by action or omission, directly or indirectly, explicitly or implicitly, discrimination, exclusion or difference based on race, religion, nationality, ideology, political, philosophical or trade union opinion, sex, gender, sexual orientation, economic position, social status, level of education or physical characteristics.
- Incitement, directly or indirectly, to violence or behavior contrary to the legal system.
- Manifestations that undermine, hinder or disrupt public policies or any action legitimately carried out by another public authority in the exercise of its powers.

– Misleading, subliminal and/or covert information.
– Include phrases, symbols, logos, color and any other element identifiable or confusing to political parties or groups, except in the case of disclosure of historical events for cultural purposes.

399. In order to receive official advertising, the media must be registered with the National Registry of Official Advertising Providers (RENAPPO) and Telam SE.

Chapter 5. Advertising Rules

§1. Various Forms of Commercial Communications

400. The licensees or authorized persons of PSB may broadcast advertising in accordance with the following provisions (Media Law 26,522, section 81):

(a) Advertisements must be nationally produced when they are broadcast by open broadcasting services or on the channels or signals of subscription services or inserted in national signals.
(b) In the case of subscription television services, they may only insert advertising in the signal corresponding to the channel of their own generation.
(c) In the case of the retransmission of open TV signals, it will not be possible to include an advertising session except for those subscription services located in the primary coverage area of the open signal.
(d) The signals transmitted by subscription services may only have the advertising session times provided for in the Media Lay (section 82) through direct contracting with each licensee and/ or authorized person.
(e) They will be broadcast with the same audio volume and must be separated from the rest of the programming.
(f) Subliminal advertising will not be broadcast, which is understood as having the ability to produce unconscious stimuli presented below the absolute sensory threshold.
(g) The stipulations for the use of the language and the protection of the minor will be complied with.
(h) Advertising aimed at girls and boys should not encourage the purchase of products by exploiting their inexperience and credulity.
(i) The advertisements will not import discrimination based on race, ethnicity, gender, sexual orientation, ideological, socioeconomic or nationality, among others; they will not undermine human dignity; they will not offend moral or religious convictions; they will not induce behaviors harmful to the environment or the physical and moral health of children and teenagers.
(j) Advertising that encourages the consumption of alcoholic beverages or tobacco or their manufacturers may only be carried out in accordance with the legal restrictions that affect those products.
(k) Programs dedicated exclusively to the promotion or sale of products may only be broadcast on the signals of ACS expressly authorized for this purpose by the enforcement authority and in accordance with the corresponding regulations.
(l) Advertisements, notices and advertising messages promoting aesthetic treatments and/ or activities related to professional practice in the health area must have the authorization of the competent authority to be disseminated and be fully in accordance with legal restrictions that affect those products or services.
(m) The advertising of games of chance must have the prior authorization of the competent authority.

(n) The implementation of a systematized control mechanism that facilitates the verification of its effective issuance.
(o) Each television advertising batch must begin and end with the identifying sign of the channel or signal in order to distinguish it from the rest of the programming.
(p) The broadcasting of advertising must respect professional concerns.
(q) Advertising programs for products, infomercials and others of a similar nature may not be counted for the purposes of complying with their own programming quotas, but they must comply with the guidelines set by the enforcement authority for their broadcast.

401. The issuance of messages of public interest provided by the Federal Authority for Audiovisual Communication Services and the issuance of the distinctive signal, as well as the legal conditions of sale or portion required by the consumer protection law, will not be counted as advertising (section 81).

402. The advertising broadcast time is subject to the following conditions (section 82):

(a) Sound broadcasting: up to a maximum of fourteen minutes per hour of broadcast.
(b) Open television: up to a maximum of twelve minutes per broadcast hour.
(c) Television by subscription; licensees may insert advertising in their own generation signal, up to a maximum of eight minutes per hour. The signal registry holders may insert up to a maximum of six minutes per hour. Advertising may only be inserted in the signals that make up the basic subscription for subscription services. The signal holders must agree with the subscription service holders the consideration for said advertising.
(d) In subscription-based ACS, in the case of signals that reach the public through devices that require an additional payment not included in the basic service, advertising may not be inserted.
(e) The enforcement authority may determine the conditions for the insertion of advertising in the audiovisual artistic works of plot unit; respecting the integrality of the narrative unit.
(f) The licensees and rights holders of the signals may accumulate the maximum hourly limit set in blocks of up to four hours per programming day. In ACS, the maximum authorized time does not include the promotion of one's own programming. These contents will not be counted within the percentages of own production required in this law. The broadcasting of programs dedicated exclusively to teleshopping and the promotion or advertising of products and services must be authorized by the enforcement authority. The regulations will establish the conditions for the insertion of promotions, sponsorships and advertising within the programs (section 82).

403. Any investment in advertising broadcasted via PSB that does not comply with the condition of a national signal will be excluded from the Income Tax reduction (section 83).

§2. RESTRICTIONS ON CONTENT

404. Those who produce, distribute, broadcast or in any way obtain benefits from the transmission of programs and/ or advertising shall ensure compliance with the provisions of laws 23,344 on tobacco advertising, 24,788—National Law to combat Alcoholism— 25,280, which approves the Inter-American Convention for the Elimination of All Forms of Discrimination against Persons with Disabilities, 25,926, on guidelines for the dissemination of health-related issues, 26,485—Integral protection law to prevent, punish, and eradicate violence against women in the areas in which they develop their interpersonal relationships—and 26,061, on comprehensive protection of the rights of girls, boys and adolescents as well as their complementary and/ or modifying norms and the norms that are dictated to health protection and protection against discriminatory behavior (section 71).

I. Right to Access Contents of Relevant Interest

405. The right to universal access is guaranteed—through PSB—to informative content of relevant interest and to sporting events, football matches or any other genre or specialty. The National Executive Power will adopt the regulatory measures so that the exercise of exclusive rights for the retransmission or television broadcast of certain events of general interest of any nature, such as sports, does not harm the right of citizens to follow said events live and free of charge, throughout the national territory. In compliance with these provisions, the Federal Council for Audiovisual Communication must prepare an annual list of events of general interest for broadcasting or television broadcasting, in respect of which the exercise of exclusive rights must be fair, reasonable and nondiscriminatory.

406. Said list will be prepared after giving a public hearing to the interested parties, with the participation of the Public Defender of Audiovisual Communication Services. The list will be prepared annually with an anticipation of at least six months and may be reviewed by the Federal Council of Audiovisual Communication under the conditions established by the regulations (section 77).

407. For inclusion in the list of events of general interest, at least the following criteria must be taken into account: (a) the event has been traditionally broadcast or broadcast on open television; (b) its performance arouses relevant attention to the television audience; (c) it is an event of national importance or a relevant international event with the participation of Argentine representatives in significant quality or quantity (section 78).

408. The transfer of rights for retransmission or broadcast, whether exclusively or not of such a nature, cannot limit or restrict the right to information. Such a situation of restriction and the concentration of exclusivity rights should not condition the normal development of the competition or affect the financial stability and independence of the clubs. In order to exercise these rights effectively, the holders of radio or television stations will have free access to the closed areas where they are to be produced. The exercise of the right of access referred to in the previous paragraph, when it comes to obtaining news or images for the broadcast of brief extracts freely chosen in news programs, will not be subject to economic consideration when they are broadcast on television and, have a maximum duration of three minutes for each event or, where appropriate, sports competition, and may not be broadcast live. The radio informational spaces will not be subject to the time and live limitations contemplated in the previous paragraph. The retransmission or total or partial broadcast by radio stations of sporting events may not be the subject of exclusive rights (section 80).

Part IV. Supervision: Media Regulator

Chapter 1. Organization

409. The ENACOM is in charge of regulating and supervising the media market in Argentina. ENACOM is an autonomous and decentralized entity that operates within the framework of the Office of the Chief of Cabinet of Ministers of the Nation. Its objective is to lead the technological convergence process and create stable market conditions to guarantee access to Internet, fixed and mobile telephony, radio, postal and television services for all Argentines. ENACOM was created in December 2015 through Decree 267 which establishes its role as communications regulator to ensure that all users in the country have quality services organized through a board of directors headed by the President of ENACOM's several directorates, according to the organization chart provided in its official site:

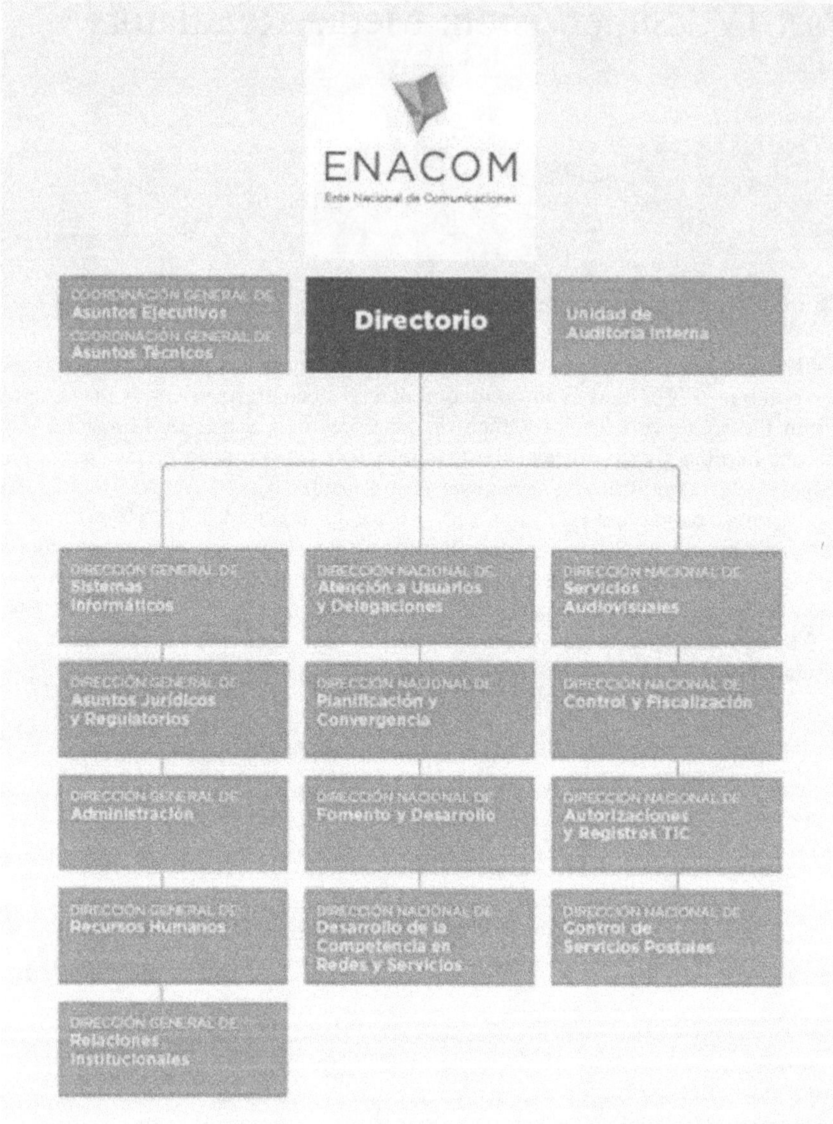

Source: ENACOM.

Chapter 2. Tasks

410. ENACOM's mission is to promote full digital inclusion, providing the entire population with access to the opportunities offered by Information and Communications Technologies, generating greater balance and competition among the different market players, streamlining its development, safeguarding the due defense of users and promoting the provision of services with high quality standards, in the context of an active regulator that strengthens the regulatory and institutional framework, ensuring that the plurality of voices and the benefits of the information society are available to all those who live in the national territory, especially those who live in rural, extreme and low-income areas. Pursuant to Article 12 of Law 26,522, ENACOM is in charge of the following tasks:

(1) To apply, interpret and enforce compliance with the present law and regulatory standards.
(2) To prepare and approve the regulations governing the operation of the Board of Directors.
(3) To be part of the representations of the National State before the corresponding international organizations and to participate in the drafting and negotiation of international treaties, agreements or conventions on broadcasting and telecommunications insofar as they may affect the provisions of this law and those referring to the processes related to the projects of the Information and Knowledge Society, when appropriate in conjunction with other state authorities with thematic competences.
(4) To prepare and update the National Service Standard and the technical standards that regulate the activity, together with the regulatory authority and the telecommunications enforcement authority.
(5) To promote the participation of ACS in the development of the Information and Knowledge Society.
(6) To approve the technical projects of broadcasting stations, grant the corresponding authorization and approve the start of regular transmissions, together with the regulatory authority and the telecommunications enforcement authority.
(7) To prepare and approve the bidding terms and conditions for the awarding of ACS.
(8) To substantiate the procedures for tenders, direct awarding and authorization, as the case may be, for the operation of ACS, keep updated the public consultation registers created by this law, which shall be published on the Internet site of the Federal Authority of Audiovisual Communication Services media possible, in order to favor the exercise of the human right to freedom of expression and communication.
(9) To award and extend, in appropriate cases, and declare the expiration of licenses, permits and authorizations, subject to full and timely judicial control, including precautionary.
(10) To supervise and verify compliance with the obligations set forth herein and the commitments assumed by the providers of audiovisual communication and broadcasting services in technical, legal, administrative and content aspects.

(11) To promote and stimulate competition and investment in the sector. To prevent and discourage monopolistic practices, anticompetitive, predatory and/or abuse of dominant position conducts within the framework of the functions assigned to this agency or others with competence in the matter.
(12) To apply the corresponding sanctions for noncompliance with this law, its regulations and administrative acts, under full and timely judicial control, including precautionary measures stations and/or broadcasts and promote the consequent judicial action, including precautionary; adopting the necessary measures to achieve the cessation of the broadcasts declared illegal.
(13) To supervise, collect and manage funds from taxes, fees and fines and to manage the assets and resources of the agency.
(14) To resolve in administrative instances the appeals and claims of the public or other interested parties.
(15) To modify, on legal or technical grounds, the technical parameters assigned to a license, permit or authorization, by the registered services.
(16) To guarantee respect for the National Constitution, laws and international treaties in the contents broadcast by ACS.
(17) To maintain and update the public records referred to herein.
(18) To register and qualify the technical and voice-over personnel working in the broadcasting and ACS when appropriate, as well as to provide for their training and qualification.
(19) To receive in its delegations and channel the presentations addressed to the Public Defender's Office.
(20) To create and administer the Hierarchical Fund for the personnel assigned to its operation.
(21) To provide the necessary resources for the operation of the Federal Council of Audiovisual Communication.
(22) To exercise its administrative and technical management.
(23) To establish its organizational and functional structure.
(24) To prepare the annual budget of expenses, the calculation of resources and the investment account.
(25) To accept subsidies, legacies and donations.
(26) To purchase, encumber and sell movable and immovable property in accordance with the regulations in force.
(27) To enter into all kinds of contracts and reciprocity agreements or agreements for the rendering of services with other agencies, entities, individuals or legal entities, pursuant to the regulations in force.
(28) To contract credits in accordance with the provisions of the regulations in force.
(29) To appoint, promote and remove its personnel.
(30) To issue the regulations, resolutions and procedural rules that may be necessary for the best performance of its functions.
(31) To respond to the requirements of the Federal Council of Audiovisual Communication, the Ombudsman and the Bicameral Commission for the Promotion and Monitoring of Audiovisual Communication.

Chapter 3. Sanctioning Powers

411. Pursuant to Article 103 of Law 26,522, failure to comply with the obligations set forth in said law, its regulations or the awarding conditions shall give rise to the application of the following minimum and maximum penalties:

(1) For privately managed for profit or not-for-profit providers, for authorized non-state providers and for the holders of the registries regulated in the present law:
  (a) Warnings.
  (b) A fine of 0.1% to 10% of the advertising turnover obtained in the month prior to the commission of the punishable act. The instrument by means of which the fine is determined shall be enforceable.
  Suspension of advertising.
  (c) Expiration of the license or registration.
  For the purposes of this subsection—in the case of legal entities—the members of the governing bodies are liable to be held responsible and sanctioned;
(2) For the administrators of state-owned broadcasting stations:
  (a) Call to attention.
  (b) Warning fine, which shall be in the personal capacity of the offending official. The instrument by which the fine is determined shall have the character of an enforceable title.
  (c) Disqualification.

Selected Bibliography

Overview

Glenn Postolski, Ana Santucho & Daniel Rodríguez. *Concentración de los medios de comunicación en Argentina: crisis y dependencia*, paper available at https://www.iade.org.ar/noticias/concentracion-de-los-medios-de-comunicacion-en-argentina-crisis-y-dependencia.

Media Owvership Montor. *Quiénes son los dueños de los medios en Argentina?*, availabe at https://argentina.mom-rsf.org/es/.

Observatorio de Medios—Unión de Trabajadores de Prensa de Buenos Aires (UTPBA)—Revista Digital N°1—año 2003.

Observatorio de Medios—Unión de Trabajadores de Prensa de Buenos Aires (UTPBA)—Revista Digital N°1—año 2003.

Infraestructure

Media Ownership Monitor. *Media Consumption*, available at https://argentina.mom-rsf.org/en/context/media-consumption/.

Instituo Nacional de Estadísticas y Censos (INDEC), information available at https://www.indec.gob.ar/indec/web/Institucional-Indec-InformesTecnicos-71.

Instituo Nacional de Estadísticas y Censos (INDEC), information available at https://www.indec.gob.ar/indec/web/Institucional-Indec-InformesTecnicos-71.

Instituo Nacional de Estadísticas y Censos (INDEC), information available at https://www.indec.gob.ar/indec/web/Institucional-Indec-InformesTecnicos-71.

Instituo Nacional de Estadísticas y Censos (INDEC), information available at https://encuestadeconsumo.sinca.gob.ar/.

Instituo Nacional de Estadísticas y Censos (INDEC), information available at https://www.sinca.gob.ar/mapa.aspx.

Freedom of Speech Right

Agustín del Cambo. *Argentina: Current Trends in Freedom of Expression Jurisprudence*, available at https://globalfreedomofexpression.columbia.edu/publications/argentina-current-trends-in-freedom-of-expression-jurisprudence/.

Selected Bibliography

Del Campo. *Calumnias e Injurias: La Situación en el fuero civil después de la ley 26551*, CELE, June 2013, available at: http://www.palermo.edu/cele/pdf/Calumnias-Injurias-Fuero-Civil.pdf.

Supreme Court, Ariel Bernardo c/Warley, Jorge A. s/daños y perjuicios, Fallos, S.755.XLVI., 1/8/13.

Supreme Court, Canicoba Corral, Rodolfo Arístides c/Acevedo, Sergio Edgardo y otros s/daños y perjuicios, Fallos: C. 1079; XLV., 14/8/13.

Supreme Court, Grupo Clarín SA y otros c/Poder Ejecutivo Nacional y otros/acción meramente declarativa, Fallos, G. 439. XLIX. (REX); G. 445. XLIX.; G. 451. XLIX.

Supreme Court, Arte Radiotelevisivo Argentino S. A. c/Estado Nacional—JGM—SMC s/amparo ley 16.986. Fallos, A. 925. XLIX., 11/2/14.

E. Bertoni y A. Del Campo. *Calumnias e Injurias, A dos Años de la Reforma del Codigo Penal Argentino,* CELE, September 2012, available at http://www.palermo.edu/cele/pdf/Calumnias-e-Injurias.pdf.

Supreme Court, Patitó, José Angel y otro c/Diario La Nación y otros, Fallos: 331:1530.

Supreme Court, Campillay, Julio César c/La Razón y otros, Fallos: 308:789.

Da Cunha Virginia c/Yahoo de Argentina SRL y Otros/daños y perjuicios—S.C., D.544, L.XLVI.

Supreme Court, Patitó, José Angel y otro c/Diario La Nación y otros, Fallos: 331:1530.

Spreme Court, Grupo Clarín SA y otros c/Poder Ejecutivo Nacional y otros/acción meramente declarativa, Fallos, G. 439. XLIX. (REX); G. 445. XLIX.; G. 451. XLIX.

Supreme Court, Editorial Río Negro S.A c/Neuquén, Provincia del s/acción de amparo, Fallos, 330:3907.

Supreme Court, Editorial Perfil S.A. y otro c/E.N.—Jefatura Gabinete de Ministros—SMC s/amparo ley 16.986, Fallos, 334:109.

Journalist Profession

Martín Becerra & Guillermo Mastrini. *Transformaciones en el sistema de medios en la Argentina del siglo XXI,* Plataforma Democtrática, July 21, 2011.

Adriana Amado Suárez. *Periodismo argentino: en busca de datos sobre la profesión*, Austral Comunicación, Volumen 1 número 2—diciembre de 2012—ISSN 2313-9137.

Miguel Ángel de Marco. *Historia del periodismo argentino: desde los orígenes hasta el centenario de Mayo*, Educa, Buenos Aires, 2006. https://repositorio.uca.edu.ar/bitstream/123456789/7909/1/historia-periodismo-argentino-desde-origenes.pdf.

Alejandro Córdoba Sosa & Mirta Luisa Jurio. *El "secreto de las fuentes" en el Sistema Interamericano de Derechos Humanos*, Revista Anales de la Facultad de Ciencias Jurídicas y Sociales. UNLP. Año 13/ Nº 46—2016. ISSN 0075-7411.

Adrián Oscar Morea. *Alcances y límites del secreto periodístico*, SAIJ, April 3, 2014. alcances_limites_secreto_periodistico.htm.

Reply Right

Marcela I. Basterra. *Derecho a la intimidad, privacidad y confidencialidad en la Ciudad Autónoma de Buenos Aires*, available at http://marcelabasterra.com.ar/wp-content/uploads/2016/11/El-rol-de-la-publicidad-oficial-en-el-marco-de-las-campan%CC%83as-electorales.-Comentario-ADC-c.-Estado-Nacional.pdf.

Access to Public Information

Santiago Díaz Cafferata. *El Derecho de Acceso a la Información Pública: Situación actual y propuestas para una Ley*, available at Ahttp://www.derecho.uba.ar/publicaciones/lye/revistas/86/06-ensayo-diaz-cafferata.pdf.

Political Broadcasting

Marcela I. Basterra. *Derecho a la intimidad, privacidad y confidencialidad en la Ciudad Autónoma de Buenos Aires*, available at http://marcelabasterra.com.ar/wp-content/uploads/2016/11/El-rol-de-la-publicidad-oficial-en-el-marco-de-las-campan%CC%83as-electorales.-Comentario-ADC-c.-Estado-Nacional.pdf.

Index

The numbers here refer to paragraph numbers.

Index

www.ingramcontent.com/pod-product-compliance
Lightning Source LLC
Chambersburg PA
CBHW071350230926
51846CB00002B/492
* 9 7 8 9 4 0 3 5 4 0 0 8 5 *